EXTERIOR House Trim

EXTERIOR House Trim

Steve Willson

CREATIVE HOMEOWNER®, Upper Saddle River, New Jersey

CREATIVE HOMEOWNER®

A Division of Federal Marketing Corp.
Upper Saddle River, NJ

EXTERIOR HOUSE TRIM
PROJECT EDITOR: Fran J. Donegan
EDITORIAL ASSISTANT: Jennifer Calvert
PHOTO RESEARCHER: Robyn Poplasky
COPY EDITOR: Elizabeth Degenhard
INDEXER: Schroeder Indexing Services
LAYOUT AND DESIGN: David Geer
ILLUSTRATIONS: Mario Ferro, George Retseck (ch. 1)
FRONT COVER PHOTOGRAPHY: *main* Brian Vanden Brink; *bottom row left to right* Brian Vanden Brink; melabee m miller; Jessie Walker; Brian Vanden Brink
BACK COVER PHOTOGRAPHY: *top right* Bob Greenspan; *bottom right* Brian Vanden Brink; *left* Mark Samu

CREATIVE HOMEOWNER
VP/ EDITORIAL DIRECTOR: Timothy O. Bakke
PRODUCTION MANAGER: Kimberly H. Vivas
ART DIRECTOR: David Geer
MANAGING EDITOR: Fran J. Donegan

Manufactured in the United States of America

Current Printing (last digit)
10 9 8 7 6 5 4 3 2 1

Exterior House Trim, First Edition
Library of Congress Control Number: 2006924727
ISBN-10: 1-58011-319-2
ISBN-13: 978-1-58011-319-9

CREATIVE HOMEOWNER®
A Division of Federal Marketing Corp.
24 Park Way, Upper Saddle River, NJ 07458
www.creativehomeowner.com

Metric Equivalents

Length

1 inch	25.4 mm
1 foot	0.3048 m
1 yard	0.9144 m
1 mile	1.61 km

Area

1 square inch	645 mm^2
1 square foot	0.0929 m^2
1 square yard	0.8361 m^2
1 acre	4046.86 m^2
1 square mile	2.59 km^2

Volume

1 cubic inch	16.3870 cm^3
1 cubic foot	0.03 m^3
1 cubic yard	0.77 m^3

Common Lumber Equivalents

Sizes: Metric cross sections are so close to their U.S. sizes, as noted below, that for most purposes they may be considered equivalents.

Dimensional lumber	1 × 2	19 × 38 mm
	1 × 4	19 × 89 mm
	2 × 2	38 × 38 mm
	2 × 4	38 × 89 mm
	2 × 6	38 × 140 mm
	2 × 8	38 × 184 mm
	2 × 10	38 × 235 mm
	2 × 12	38 × 286 mm
Sheet sizes	4 × 8 ft.	1200 × 2400 mm
	4 × 10 ft.	1200 × 3000 mm
Sheet thicknesses	¼ in.	6 mm
	⅜ in.	9 mm
	½ in.	12 mm
	¾ in.	19 mm
Stud/joist spacing	16 in. o.c.	400 mm o.c.
	24 in. o.c.	600 mm o.c.

Capacity

1 fluid ounce	29.57 mL
1 pint	473.18 mL
1 quart	0.95 L
1 gallon	3.79 L

Weight

1 ounce	28.35g
1 pound	0.45kg

Temperature

Fahrenheit = Celsius × 1.8 + 32
Celsius = Fahrenheit – 32 × 5⁄9

Nail Size & Length

Penny Size	Nail Length
2d	1"
3d	1¼"
4d	1½"
5d	1¾"
6d	2"
7d	2¼"
8d	2½"
9d	2¾"
10d	3"
12d	3¼"
16d	3½"

SAFETY

Although the methods in this book have been reviewed for safety, it is not possible to overstate the importance of using the safest methods you can. What follows are reminders—some do's and don'ts of work safety—to use along with your common sense.

- *Always* use caution, care, and good judgment when following the procedures described in this book.
- *Always* be sure that the electrical setup is safe, that no circuit is overloaded, and that all power tools and outlets are properly grounded. Do not use power tools in wet locations.
- *Always* read container labels on paints, solvents, and other products; provide ventilation; and observe all other warnings.
- *Always* read the manufacturer's instructions for using a tool, especially the warnings.
- Use hold-downs and push sticks whenever possible when working on a table saw. Avoid working short pieces if you can.
- *Always* remove the key from any drill chuck (portable or press) before starting the drill.
- *Always* pay deliberate attention to how a tool works so that you can avoid being injured.
- *Always* know the limitations of your tools. Do not try to force them to do what they were not designed to do.
- *Always* make sure that any adjustment is locked before proceeding. For example, always check the rip fence on a table saw or the bevel adjustment on a portable saw before starting to work.
- *Always* clamp small pieces to a bench or other work surface when using a power tool.
- *Always* wear the appropriate rubber gloves or work gloves when handling chemicals, moving or stacking lumber, working with concrete, or doing heavy construction.
- *Always* wear a disposable face mask when you create dust by sawing or sanding. Use a special filtering respirator when working with toxic substances and solvents.
- *Always* wear eye protection, especially when using power tools or striking metal on metal or concrete; a chip can fly off, for example, when chiseling concrete.
- *Never* work while wearing loose clothing, hanging hair, open cuffs, or jewelry.

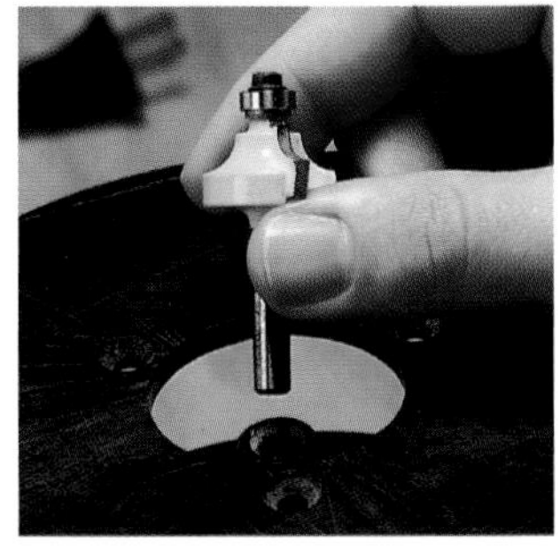

- *Always* be aware that there is seldom enough time for your body's reflexes to save you from injury from a power tool in a dangerous situation; everything happens too fast. Be alert!
- *Always* keep your hands away from the business ends of blades, cutters, and bits.
- *Always* hold a circular saw firmly, usually with both hands.
- *Always* use a drill with an auxiliary handle to control the torque when using large-size bits.
- *Always* check your local building codes when planning new construction. The codes are intended to protect public safety and should be observed to the letter.
- *Never* work with power tools when you are tired or under the influence of alcohol or drugs.
- *Never* cut tiny pieces of wood or pipe using a power saw. When you need a small piece, saw it from a securely clamped longer piece.
- *Never* change a saw blade or a drill or router bit unless the power cord is unplugged. Do not depend on the switch being off. You might accidentally hit it.
- *Never* work in insufficient lighting.
- *Never* work with dull tools. Have them sharpened, or learn how to sharpen them yourself.
- *Never* use a power tool on a workpiece—large or small—that is not firmly supported.
- *Never* saw a workpiece that spans a large distance between horses without close support on each side of the cut; the piece can bend, closing on and jamming the blade, causing saw kickback.
- When sawing, *never* support a workpiece from underneath with your leg or other part of your body.
- *Never* carry sharp or pointed tools, such as utility knives, awls, or chisels, in your pocket. If you want to carry these tools, use a special-purpose tool belt that has leather pockets and holders.

CONTENTS

8 INTRODUCTION

CHAPTER 1

12 UNDERSTANDING HOUSE STYLES

14 GEORGIAN STYLE 1720–1780
16 FEDERAL STYLE 1790–1830
18 GREEK REVIVAL STYLE 1820–1860
20 VICTORIAN STYLES
• Italianate Style 1840–1890 • Queen Anne Style 1860–1910
24 SHINGLE STYLE 1880–1910
26 COLONIAL REVIVAL STYLE 1880–1940
28 ARTS AND CRAFTS STYLE 1890–1920
30 MODERN STYLE 1920–1960

CHAPTER 2

32 TRIMWORK FOR ROOFS

34 RAKE TRIM
36 GABLE OVERHANGS
• Bargeboards
40 FASCIA AND SOFFIT TRIMWORK
42 DORMERS
44 CUPOLAS
46 ROOF VENTING TRIM

CHAPTER 3

48 ENTRY DETAILS

50 DOORS AND CASINGS
52 FRONT DOOR OPTIONS
56 SCREEN DOORS
58 PEDIMENTS AND HEAD CASINGS
60 ADDING GLASS
• Transom Windows
64 PORTICOES
68 PERGOLAS
70 PORTE COCHERES

CHAPTER 4

72 WINDOW AND WALL TRIM

74 WINDOW CASINGS
78 SHUTTERS
80 CORNER BOARDS
82 FRIEZES
84 DECORATIVE FRIEZES
86 WATER TABLES
88 PILASTERS, BRACKETS, AND OTHER ELEMENTS

CHAPTER 5

90 PORCHES

92 COLUMNS
94 CAPITAL IDEAS
96 PORCH RAILINGS
100 PORCH CEILINGS
102 PORCH FLOORS
104 DECORATIVE TRIMWORK

106 PIER SCREENS
108 PORCH STEPS
110 ENCLOSED PORCHES
112 FLOOR FRAMING

CHAPTER 6
114 TRIMWORK FOR OUTBUILDINGS
116 GARAGES
118 STORAGE SHEDS
120 DECORATIVE OUTBUILDINGS
122 BARNS
124 GAZEBOS
126 GREENHOUSES
128 ARBORS

CHAPTER 7
130 HOUSE SIDING
132 WOOD CLAPBOARD
134 SHINGLES AND SHAKES
136 PLYWOOD SIDING
138 COLOR SCHEMES
140 NON-WOOD SIDING
• Aluminum Siding • Fiber-Cement Siding
146 STUCCO
148 BRICK

CHAPTER 8
150 TOOLS AND MATERIALS
152 BASIC TOOLS
• Squares • Levels • Saws • Files and Rasps • Cordless Drill/Driver • Sanding and Paint Removal • Abrasives
158 POWER CUTTING TOOLS
• Circular Saws • Jig Saws • Miter Saws • Bench-Top Table Saws • Routers/Router Tables
161 RESTORATION TOOLS
162 TRIMWORK MATERIALS
• Solid Wood Trim • Alternatives to Solid Wood • Plastic Materials • Panel Products
170 FINISHING MATERIALS
• Types of Finishes
172 PAINT

CHAPTER 9
174 MAINTENANCE AND REPAIRS
176 DIAGNOSING PROBLEMS
178 MAKING REPAIRS
180 REPLACING DAMAGED TRIMWORK
182 RESTORATION OR REPLACEMENT?
184 PORCH RAILINGS AND FLOORS
186 COLUMN RESTORATION
188 PAINTING
190 ROUTINE MAINTENANCE

192 RESOURCE GUIDE
198 GLOSSARY
202 INDEX
207 CREDITS

INTRODUCTION

THE AMERICAN HOUSING STOCK is packed full of different architectural styles. It's not hard to find a stunning example of Italianate design just down the road from a vernacular farmhouse that offers little more than four walls and a gable roof. This diversity is one of the enduring charms of American architecture, and it exists from sea to shining sea, in big places like New York, Chicago, and Los Angeles and in smaller ones like Montgomery, Little Rock, and Amarillo, too. Their best streets are like architecture labs. Within a few blocks you can see well-bred examples of Colonial Revival, Queen Anne, Greek Revival, and Modern homes, all part of a vibrant and beautiful neighborhood.

DETAILS MAKE A DIFFERENCE. The roof trim shown **above** adds distinction to this house.

EVEN THE SIMPLEST DESIGNS, right, grow in stature with the addition of the right trimwork.

You will also find houses that consist of a mixture of styles. In fact, many of the houses lining our streets are difficult to place in a specific category. Designers and builders of these houses picked elements they liked from one design style and applied it to another, helping to create the diversity of house styles around us. If you're interested in architecture and architectural trimwork, get in your car and take a drive through one of these neighborhoods. This is a great way to refine your taste. With so many different styles cascading past you, it's not hard to decide what you like a little and what you like a lot.

One thing you'll notice right away is that exterior trim is not purely ornamental. In fact, it is rarely just ornamental, and when it functions as ornament, it is often as an after thought. Its primary purposes are to create transitions between fields of siding and to seal vulnerable areas of the house against harmful weathering. In terms of pure design, trim derives its importance from its prominence. Because siding is almost always repetitive, it tends to be monotonous. Anything that breaks up this monotony, as trimwork does, necessarily catches the eye. Trim also plays a big role in visually outlining a house,

TRIMWORK DEFINES STYLE. In many cases, the type of trimwork used depends on the style of house, such as the bargeboard on this early Victorian.

the way simple lines define a rectangle. Corner boards form hard verticals, fascias are strong horizontals, and rake boards hold the roof to the end walls so it won't fly away.

Knowing something about trimwork can be edifying in itself, particularly if you are interested in house design. But it becomes more actionable, as they say, when you want to buy a new house or you're planning a substantial addition to your current house. Because trim is so important to the final look of a building, you'll want to be confidently involved in specifying the proper details. At the end of the day, the architect, builder, and contractors go home. Make sure what they leave behind is what you want.

This book is designed to help you in a number of ways. First, there's an overview of well known architectural styles, so you'll know what type of house you're looking at when you see it.

Then the focus moves from the general to the specific to discuss each major piece of exterior trim, including its design purpose, its

ADDING DISTINCTIVE TRIMWORK is a great way to embellish your house and express your individual style.

structural use, and how it's attached to the house. Once this is accomplished, our focus moves out again to the broader issue of different types of siding. Because the trim is always an integral part of the siding, you need to know a little bit about siding if you want to know a lot about trim.

Then comes a tutorial on the kinds of tools you'll need if you want to deal with the trim on your own house. This is followed by a roundup of the materials commonly used for exterior trim. In addition to the old standby, wood, you will also learn about the new generation of materials, as well as the wide variety of finishes that can be applied to keep your old or new trim in tip-top shape. We finish up by spending some time on simple exterior trim restoration techniques. In most cases, when a trim board needs replacement, the best approach is to match the new to the old as closely as possible. Other times, what is on a house should be improved, so you'll need some strategies for making changes—not just replacements.

ENTRY AREAS, below left, benefit from trimwork. The portico shown here adds a classic touch.

VICTORIAN DESIGNS, below right, are noted for their elaborate ornamentation and detail.

CHAPTER 1

UNDERSTANDING HOUSE STYLES

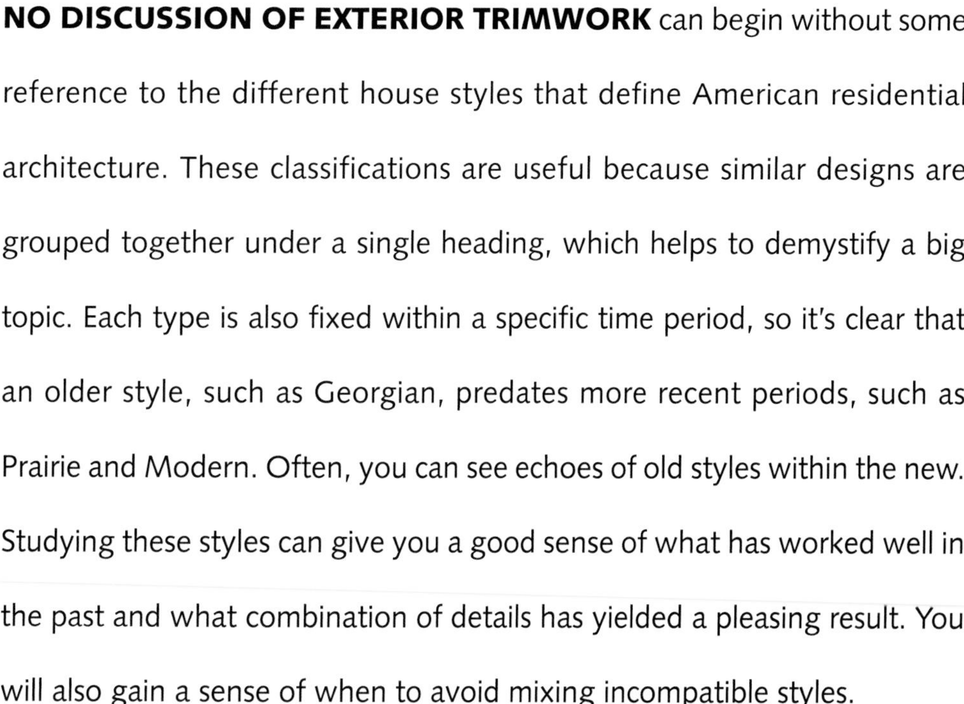

NO DISCUSSION OF EXTERIOR TRIMWORK can begin without some reference to the different house styles that define American residential architecture. These classifications are useful because similar designs are grouped together under a single heading, which helps to demystify a big topic. Each type is also fixed within a specific time period, so it's clear that an older style, such as Georgian, predates more recent periods, such as Prairie and Modern. Often, you can see echoes of old styles within the new. Studying these styles can give you a good sense of what has worked well in the past and what combination of details has yielded a pleasing result. You will also gain a sense of when to avoid mixing incompatible styles.

In this chapter, you'll find photos and drawings that show the basic tenets of each style. Does the design feature a steep roof or one with a shallow pitch? Are the windows small or large? Is the front door placed at the center of the elevation or off to one side? Elements like these, when examined closely, reveal how an attractive design is created.

GEORGIAN STYLE
1720–1780

LIKE MANY OF THE DESIGN INFLUENCES that flourished in America, the Georgian style was a British import. Named after Kings George I, II, and III—who ruled from 1714 to 1820—these designs were popular from Maine to northern Florida.

Georgian houses were usually large, two-story, rectangular-shaped buildings with front doors that almost always centered on the front elevation. These entries were elaborate, having flattened pilasters, glazed transoms above, and a pediment or decorative head casing capping the whole assembly. Later in this period, semicircular fanlights sometimes replaced the transoms and pediments.

The eaves on these houses were almost always situated above the front door and often featured decorative dentils along the cornices. The roofs were moderately to steeply pitched. But the roof shape was not nearly so predictable—hip roofs, gambrels, and side gables were all common.

Chimneys. In the New England area, these houses were usually made of wood and featured a large chimney going through the middle of the house. In the Mid-Atlantic states, wood gave way to brick or stone exteriors, and two large chimneys, one on each end of the building, replaced the single center chimney

Double-hung windows, with multipane sashes, were standard and their placement was almost always symmetrical, especially on the front of the house. Two windows on each side of the door defined the style, with the windows on the second floor placed directly above those on the first floor. All of the windows received conservative trim treatments, just simple side casings and maybe a slightly more elaborate head casing. A porch rarely appeared on the front elevation, though open porches were sometimes located on the sides of the house.

GEORGIAN-STYLE HOUSES often include pilasters as trim around the front door, **above,** and double-hung widows, **below,** with six to nine panes of glass per sash.

A TWO-STORY BUILDING with the front door in the middle of the facade is a typical Georgian-era design.

GEORGIAN STYLE

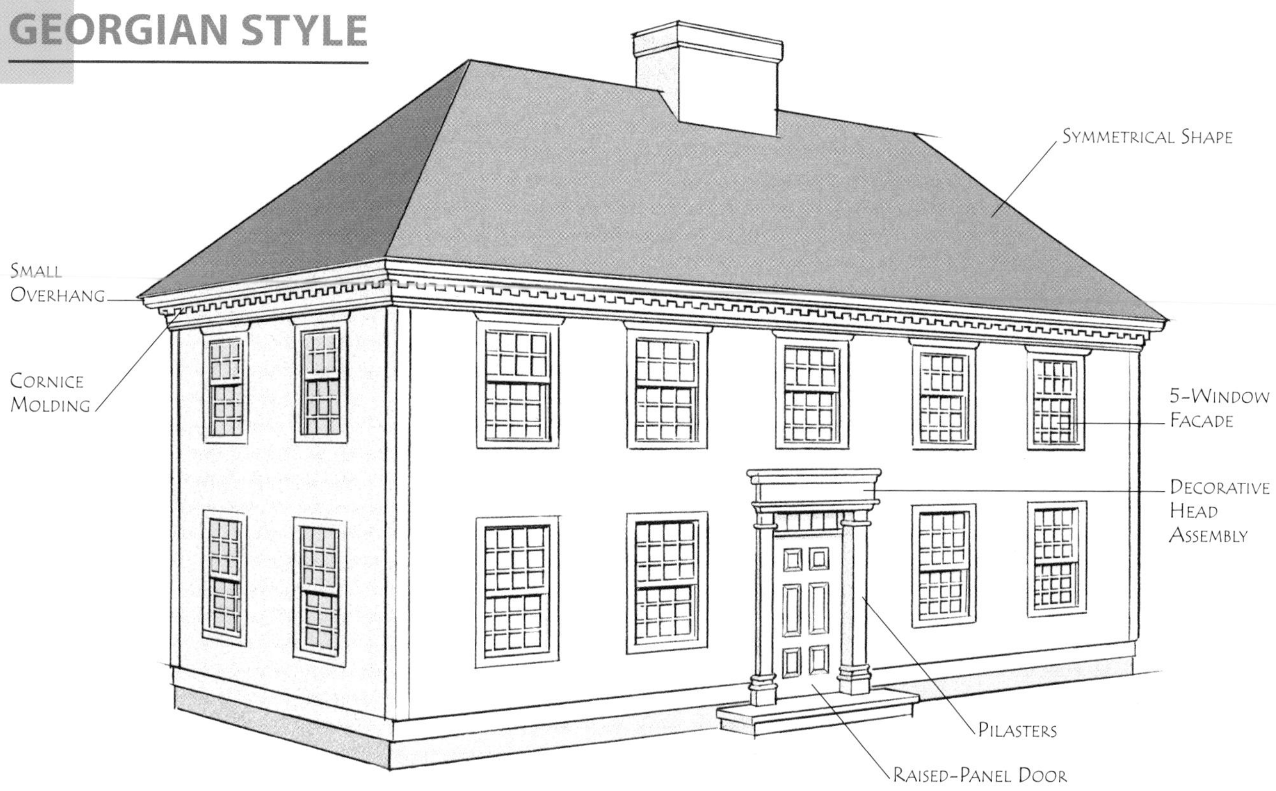

Symmetrical Shape

Small Overhang

Cornice Molding

5-Window Facade

Decorative Head Assembly

Pilasters

Raised-Panel Door

FEDERAL STYLE
1790–1830

After the American Revolution, the influence of the Georgian style started to fade and was replaced by forward-thinking architects who developed the Federal style. The changes weren't startling, but the Federal style was a refinement of the Georgian approach.

Both designs used large, boxy, two-story buildings with relatively elaborate entryways. A fanlight window above, and a sidelight on both sides, almost always flanked the Federal entrance door. When a front porch was built, it was usually a one-story, semicircular structure just slightly wider than the front door assembly. The window placement was uniform on all elevations, with the windows lining up vertically on the first and second stories. The casings around the windows were simple, except for the head casing that could sometimes be ornamental. In brick buildings, a keystone was often used in the window lentils.

Window Styles. The windows themselves were longer than those in Georgian designs, and featured larger panes of glass. This increase in size was largely due to the production of glass in the states, allowing for cheaper, more readily available glass. Windows on the first story nearly reached to the floor and louvered shutters became popular.

As in Georgian buildings, the roof on a Federal house often had end gables with the front eave placed over the front door. Hip

FEDERAL STYLE

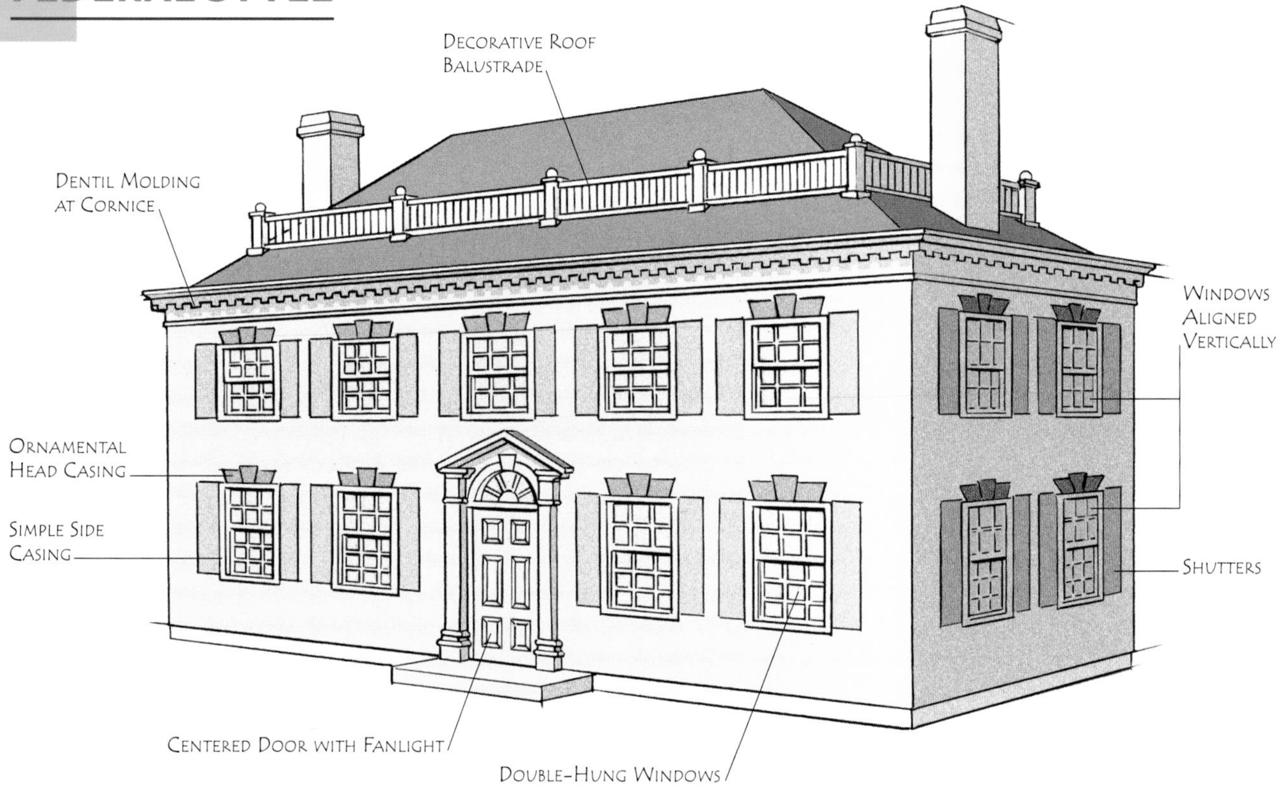

Decorative Roof Balustrade
Dentil Molding at Cornice
Windows Aligned Vertically
Ornamental Head Casing
Simple Side Casing
Shutters
Centered Door with Fanlight
Double-Hung Windows

Classical Influences

GEORGIAN, FEDERAL, AND GREEK REVIVAL style homes relied on theories of design developed by the ancient Greeks and Romans. Many of these theories deal with the size and spacing of columns and the structures they support. The column shown at right supports an entablature that consists of an architrave, frieze, and the cornice. You can find these elements in public buildings built in the classical style. Some of the components, especially columns and cornice treatments, appear in a variety of residential styles.

roofs were also very popular and sometimes featured balustrades above the roof eaves. One notable departure from the Georgian period was the roof pitch. Federal designs had lower pitches, around three or four in twelve, which made the roof look nearly flat when seen from the street.

The popularity of Federal styles spread west and south during the early nineteenth century, largely by way of detailed pattern books that were used by local builders and tradespeople. In the North, these patterns were executed in wood frame construction; in the South, masonry usually prevailed.

ENTRYWAY TRIM, opposite and below, became more elaborate during the Federal period. Note the use of fanlight, opposite, and transom windows, below.

THE TRIM AROUND THE DORMERS of this modern house, **above,** echoes the basics of Greek Revival design.

GRAND HOUSES in the Greek Revival style, **below,** often incorporate the classic gable pediment and large columns in their designs.

GREEK REVIVAL STYLE 1820–1860

THE GREEK REVIVAL STYLE captured the American imagination more than any other popular design. From churches and banks to plantation houses and farmhouses, this style took hold. Probably its most enduring contribution was the simple gable front design that may be the default rural house of the nineteenth century.

A gable end facing the street was an echo of the classic Greek temple that had a pediment over its entrance. And like the columns that supported these temples, Greek Revival designs had oversized columns that supported a large front porch. Where a porch was omitted, elaborate pilasters at the corner boards, and sometimes at regular intervals across the front elevation, suggested the temple columns.

While Georgian and Federal styles were constructed of different materials depending on the region (wood frame in the Northeast, brick in the South), the Greek Revival designs were most often post-and-beam wood structures. They were finished with clapboards that were invariably painted a bright white and outfitted with shutters.

Entrance Styles. Greek Revival entrances were elaborate. They featured multipaned sidelights and transoms (instead of fanlights), columns or pilasters on both sides of the door, and sometimes, double doors. These entries were commonly situated in the middle of the front elevation, just as in Georgian and Federal designs. But many were placed off to one side, something that rarely happened with earlier designs.

In the Greek Revival world, first floor windows reached nearly to the floor. They featured six-over-six panes or nine-over-nine double-hung sashes. On the second or sometimes third floor, small, horizontal windows were installed in the frieze just below the cornice and covered with wood or iron grilles. Typically the frieze board that surrounded these windows was very wide, made of at least two boards.

As mentioned earlier, Greek Revival designs usually featured gable roofs; but hip roofs were also popular. Both designs had shallow pitches, so there was no need for attic dormers because there wasn't enough headroom to use the attic space.

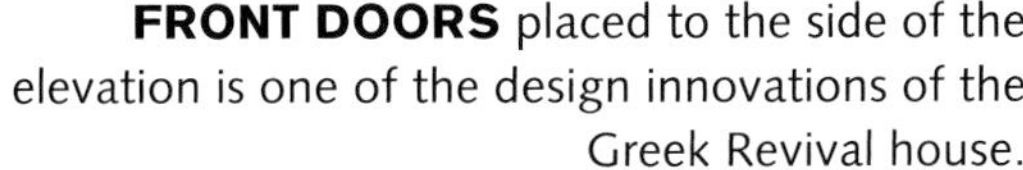

FRONT DOORS placed to the side of the elevation is one of the design innovations of the Greek Revival house.

GREEK REVIVAL STYLE

Symmetrical Shape

Wide Frieze Detail at Cornice

Gable with Pediment

Unfluted Columns

Sidelights

Entry Porch

Simple Casings

Double-Hung Windows

VICTORIAN STYLES

THERE WERE MULTIPLE VICTORIAN STYLES that spread across the United States from the middle of the nineteenth century to the middle of the twentieth. Second Empire and Romanesque Revival designs—with their remarkable mansard roofs—Italianate and Queen Anne were popular and widespread. Most of these styles borrowed heavily from one another, and many houses that we call Victorian today are really a combination of a number of specific house designs.

Italianate Style 1840–1890

In the middle of the nineteenth century, interest grew in various Italian architecture styles—especially Italianate, Villa, and Renaissance Revival. Of these, the most popular was the Italianate style, probably because it was the easiest of the three to build. Also, many of the details that are representative of the style could be appropriately added to other simple house styles.

Italianate houses are two- or three-story square boxes with low-pitched hipped roofs.

HOUSES WE LABEL AS VICTORIAN tend to include a number of elements from different Victorian designs as shown in the house at the **top of the page.**

SECOND EMPIRE VICTORIANS, center, often feature mansard roofs that are pierced by dormers or windows.

ITALIANATE-STYLE HOUSES, left, usually contain wide overhangs that appear to be supported by large brackets. Cupolas are another common feature found on these houses.

Very wide overhangs are standard and are supported with thick ornate brackets, sometimes installed in pairs. Occasionally, these ornamental brackets were replaced with large dentils.

Cupolas were very popular and were of standard pattern-book fare. They added interest to otherwise bland roofs, and in warmer climates they provided excellent ventilation. When the windows in the cupola and the house below were open, even a gentle breeze could pull out the warm air from inside the house.

Double-hung windows were the most common and tended to be narrow and high, usually with arched or curved tops. Their placement was symmetrical on all elevations, aligning horizontally and vertically with other windows and entrance doors. In brick and stucco models, the windows were topped with keystone arches. On some houses, small awning windows were placed between eave brackets and aligned with the windows on the two stories beneath them.

Porch Designs. The front elevation of an Italianate house often had an entry porch, usually the full width of the building. The support columns, railings, and stairs were less ornate during the first few decades of this style, but became more ornamented as the years went by. The entrance doors took design cues from the windows. Double doors were very popular, and they often had large panes of glass on their upper halves. If the windows had arched tops, so did the doors.

ITALIANATE STYLE

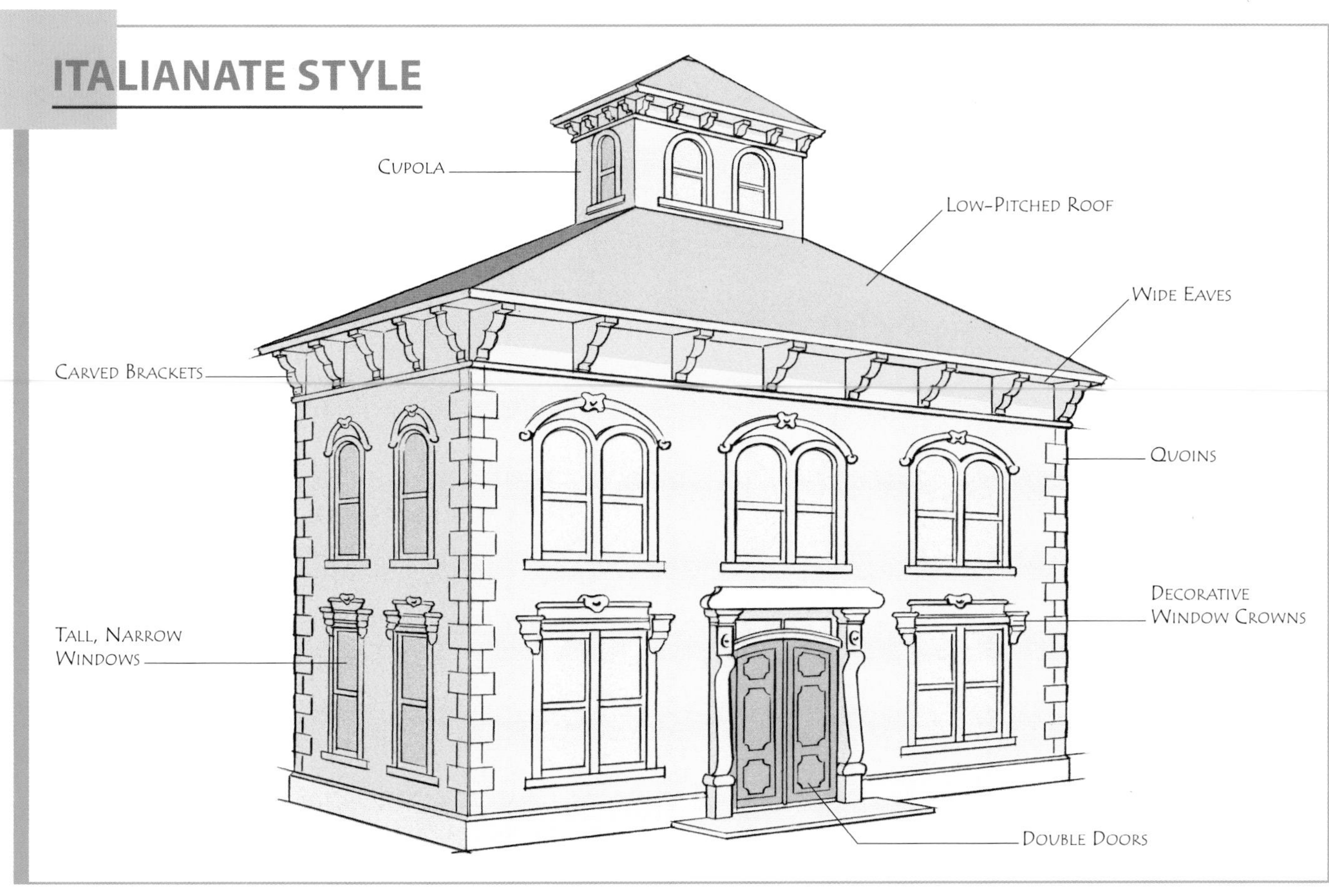

Queen Anne Style
1860–1910

Queen Anne designs were also extremely popular during the Victorian period, and wonderful examples can be found on the East and West coast and nearly every place in between. One reason for this popularity was the mail-order availability of the Queen Anne-style designs. Even though these structures were complicated, all of the parts could be precut and shipped by rail.

LAYERS OF TRIMWORK, such as the cornice and porch detains shown at **right** contribute to the look of opulence of many Victorian homes.

TOWERS AND STEEP GABLES, below, provide the Queen Anne design with its distinctive look. Although not shown here, stained glass was common.

Distinctive Elements. Queen Anne-style houses were large, old structures that had numerous angles. The roofs were made up of a cacophony of steep gables and hips, wide overhangs, and dormers. Walls in this particular style were loaded with entry porches, towers, bay windows, and prominent chimneys. Building materials similarly varied; wood clapboards, cedar shingles, brick, stone, and stucco were all used—often in a single structure.

Large, inner-city models were more characteristic of the Queen Anne style; however, smaller houses of this fashion sprung up in rural areas, in tight urban plots, and in practically every small town in the country. These versions had less complicated roofs, fewer material textures, no towers, and a single bay window instead of four or five.

Windows were large pane, double-hung models. In expensive houses, stained glass was used as a design accent in some of the sashes, particularly in windows on the first floor. Often, entry doors had large panes of glass of etched or frosted glass in place of standard, wood panels.

Color Dominates. With the emergence of the Victorian era came a forceful goodbye to the Greek Revival-style stark white house. Instead, bright colors prevailed. It was common to have six or seven different colored paints on a large Queen Anne. Another common decorative element was the use of spindles on the outside of the house. Porch columns and balusters were invariably turned into spindles, as were porch friezes (just below the ceilings) and gable decorations.

THE LACY TRIMWORK on the gable is a common element in Gothic Victorian designs.

QUEEN ANNE STYLE

Steep-Pitched Roof

Front-Facing Gable

Textured Shingles

Asymmetrical Shape

Wraparound 1-Story Porch

Ornamental Brackets

Double-Hung Windows

SHINGLE STYLE
1880–1910

IN MANY WAYS, the Shingle style is the easiest architectural design to identify, with its wood shingles covering the home from the foundation to the ridgeline. These large, two- and three-story buildings first appeared in the Northeast as summer homes for the affluent, but later the style quickly spread across the country.

A Queen Anne-style skeleton could be found underneath the shingles in this particular design. The roofs had wild combinations of hip, gable, and gambrel shapes, as well as dormers abound. Stone foundations—sometimes covering the entire first floor—and prominent chimneys were staples of the design. Large front porches and multiple projecting bay windows were also common features.

Ornamentation. Even though similarities existed between the Queen Anne and Shingle designs, they were inherently different, particularly in their ornamentation. Shingle-style windows and trim were subdued. Porch columns and balusters were plain. No spindle friezes appeared along porch ceilings, and no gable ends were decorated with gingerbread trim.

This plainness of the Shingle style was intentional and sought to smooth out the extreme texture of the Queen Anne style. The Shingle designers wanted the whole house to blend together nicely. An example of this was the lack of corner boards present at the corners

SHINGLE STYLE

Wood Shingles

Projecting Bay

Plain Columns and Railings

Large Porch

of the house—instead, the shingles wrapped around the corner, creating a different effect. This surface blending was also true of the towers that both styles featured. Queen Anne houses had full towers with separate roofs in contrast to the Shingle houses, which were likely to have smaller towers with a roof integrated into the main-roof design.

Though the Shingle style was very well known and examples of it were built in all areas of the country, this style home was never quite as popular as the Queen Anne design. Shingle houses largely remained the province of architects instead of mass builders because they were large and expensive, and looked best when placed on substantial pieces of land instead of on the tighter building lots available in cities.

SHINGLE-STYLE HOMES, opposite and above, are reminiscent of Queen Anne designs, but on a more subdued level. The large front porch and bay window shown above are common elements.

EXPOSED STONE FOUNDATIONS and minimal trimwork, **left,** are a response to the busy designs found in the Victorian era. This style of house was most popular in the Northeast.

COLONIAL REVIVAL HOMES are often based on simple, open floor plans. Note the single-pane lower sash on the windows.

COLONIAL REVIVAL STYLE 1880–1940

MANY EXPERTS CONSIDER the Colonial Revival design the most popular residential style in the history of the United States. As the name implies, these designs were reinterpretations and updates of older colonial buildings. This approach came into popularity in 1876, and examples continue to be designed and built, even today, 125 years after first appearing.

These houses are usually two- or three-stories with high-pitched side-gabled, hipped, or gambrel roofs. The eaves tended to be plain or minimally ornamented, with a string of dentils. Most designs were wood framed buildings with clapboard siding. Only in later decades did brick versions become common.

COLONIAL REVIVAL STYLE

Centered Dormer
Symmetrical Shape
Pediment
Shutters
Multipane Double-Hung Windows
Pillars or Columns
Paired Windows
Entry Door Centered in Portico

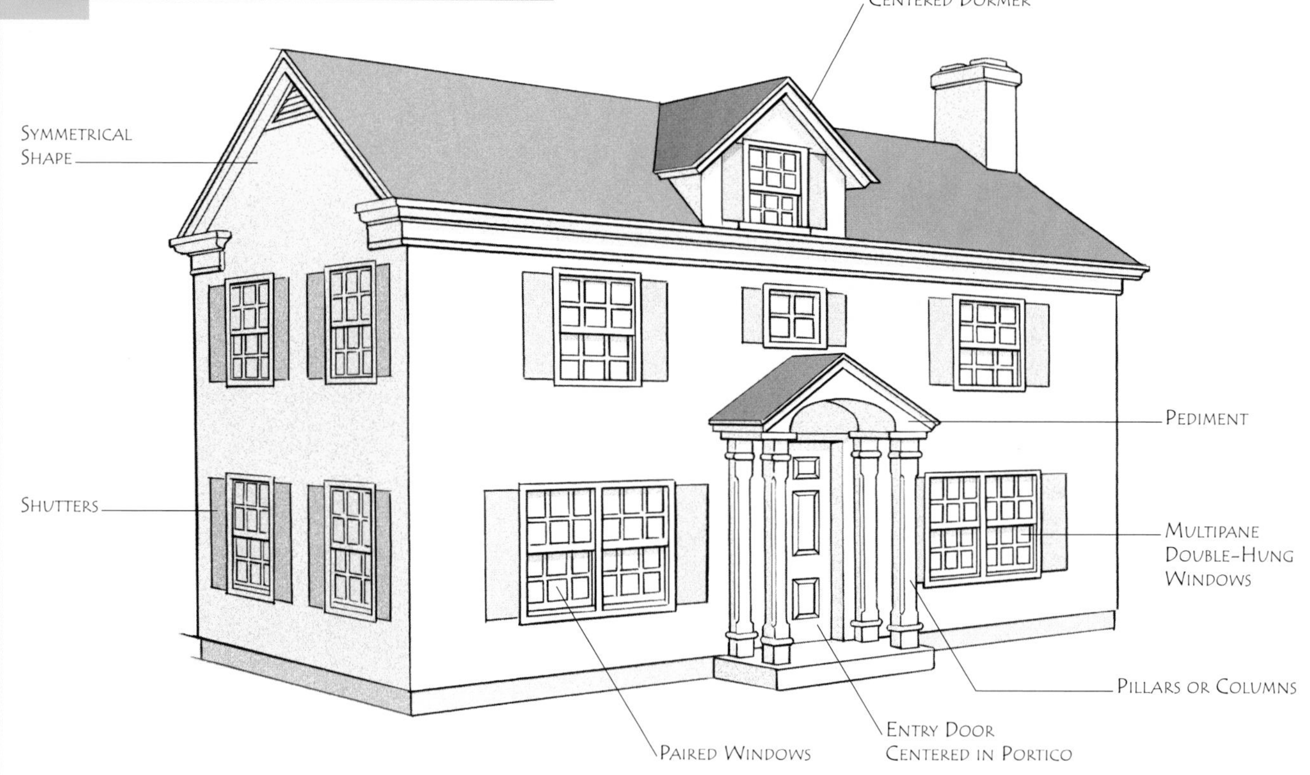

Trend-Setting Houses

HIGH-PROFILE BUILDINGS, such as Thomas Jefferson's Monticello, shown at right, have a great influence on architects and designers. In designing Monticello, Jefferson, who was not a trained architect, mixed styles to create a pleasing design because it follows established design principles. Note how the entry portico is in proportion to the house behind it and how the columns support the pediment. The doors and windows on the front facade provide a human scale that makes the whole house inviting. While most of the houses we live in are not as grand as Monticello, all houses benefit when the designers follow established design principles.

Combining Styles. Residents of this time frame preferred older, simpler architecture with newer, open floor plans and more conveniences, such as large, efficient kitchens, central heating, and multiple bathrooms. To accomplish this, designers took Georgian and Federal styles and combined them with details from other styles to arrive at something that was new, yet suggested something old.

Due to the derivative nature of this style, it's sometimes difficult to identify Colonial Revival houses. However, there are some typical identifiers. First, the double-hung windows tended to be larger than colonial models and were often installed in pairs—something that wasn't done in colonial times. A multipane upper sash installed over a single-pane lower sash was a typical Colonial Revival detail. Dormers and bay windows were very common Colonial Revival accents as well, but were never used on early colonial buildings.

Entries. Relatively elaborate entryways were also characteristic of Colonial Revival styles. Front doors, centered on the elevation had sidelights and a Palladian window above them. Small, elaborate porches with turned columns further bolstered the entryway. These houses often featured corner pilasters, less prominent chimneys, and a very popular side porch—with a balustrade above it—that was often screened in as time progressed.

DISTINCTIVE ENTRYWAYS, below, are common on Colonial Revival houses. Many feature porticos that are supported by substantial columns. Sidelights and Palladian windows are also common.

ARTS AND CRAFTS STYLE 1890–1920

The Arts and Crafts Movement began in Great Britain as a reaction to the Industrial Revolution occurring in the United States. Those advocates for the movement felt that manufactured objects were becoming characterless and poorly made. Instead, they preferred the look of hand-wrought items made of natural materials. While the movement did embrace all types of crafts, its greatest impact in the United States was in home design, as seen in three distinct housing types: Prairie, Craftsmen, and Bungalow. While each of these designs has it's own distinguishing characteristics, some elements are common to all three.

Common Characteristics. First, these houses were generally smaller than their Victorian predecessors. In turn, they cost less to build (and buy) and would fit on smaller, urban lots. Many were sold as precut kits from suppliers such as Sears Roebuck. Everything except the foundation and landscaping was included and the kits could be sent to anywhere that had a railroad station.

These designs were generally either one- or one-and-one-half story houses and were usually sided with dark-colored wood shingles, shakes, or clapboards. The roofs were either side- or front-gabled. Only rarely was a hipped roof used. No matter what orientation the roof occupied, the eaves were wide and featured exposed rafter tails. When a dormer was used, it had a gable roof, not a

ARTS AND CRAFTS STYLE

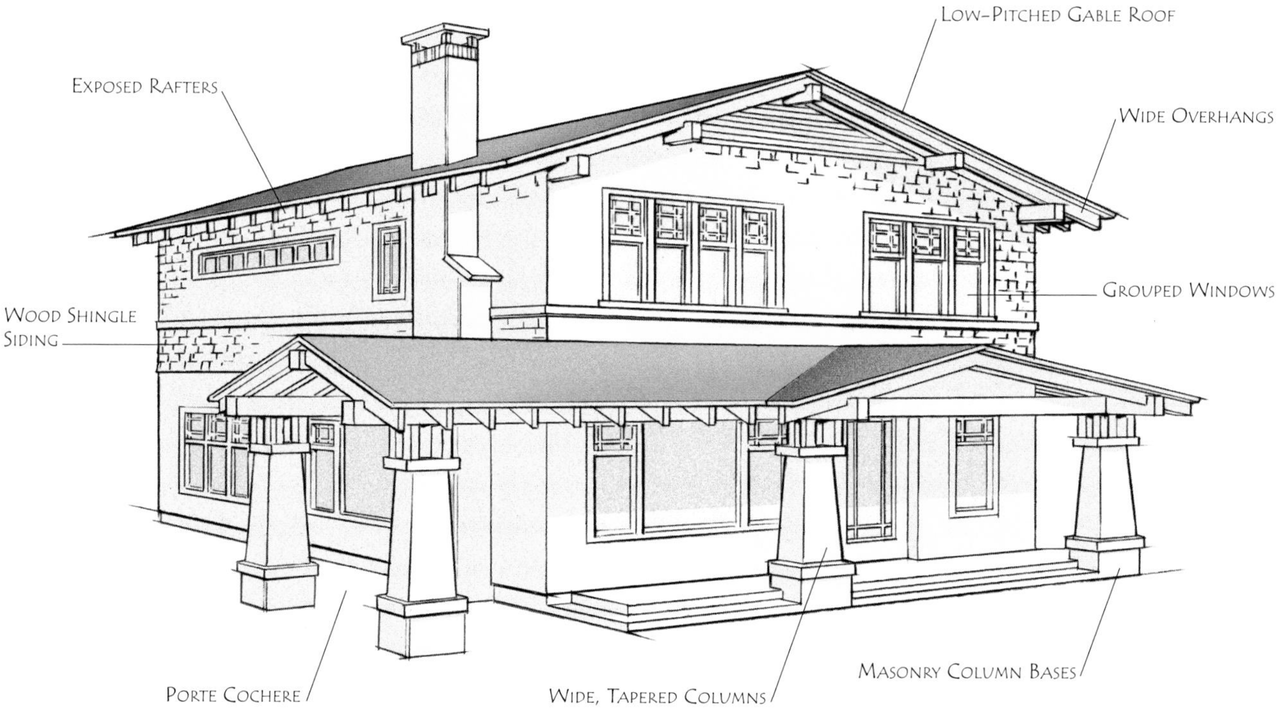

Low-Pitched Gable Roof
Exposed Rafters
Wide Overhangs
Grouped Windows
Wood Shingle Siding
Porte Cochere
Wide, Tapered Columns
Masonry Column Bases

shed roof, and the same wide overhangs and exposed rafters of the main roof.

Porches. Front porches were standard and often connected to adjacent pergolas or porte cocheres. Wide, tapered columns that extended all the way to the ground supported all of these structures. Sometimes, the bottom halves of these columns were made from local stone or brick, as were the house chimneys. When a porch was included on a side-gabled house, it was almost always placed under the main roof. The windows in most Arts and Crafts houses were double-hung and featured multipane upper sashes and single-paned lower sashes.

The most popular of all these designs was the bungalow. From 1900 to World War I, the bungalow captured the imagination of the whole country, starting in California and moving all the way to the East coast.

ARTS AND CRAFTS HOUSES, opposite, often contain columns on masonry bases. The designs avoid excessive ornamentation, **top.**

PRAIRIE-STYLE HOUSES, above, feature wide overhangs, flat roofs, and strong horizontal lines.

BUNGALOW HOMES, left, are among the most popular Arts and Crafts designs. They tend to feature large porches and front-facing gables. Note the masonry bases of the columns.

MODERN STYLE
1920–1960

THE MODERN STYLE in American residential architecture is composed of two similar styles: Art Moderne and International, both European imports. In terms of popularity, the International style prevailed. In fact, International style houses are still being designed and built by contemporary architects such as Michael Graves and Richard Meier.

HOUSES IN THE MODERN STYLE, above, are usually custom-built residences that would look out of place in the typical housing development.

THE USE OF GLASS, below, is one of the areas that sets a modern design apart from more traditional styles.

The idea behind International architecture is an emphasis on rational design, or as one famous architect described it, like "machines to live in." This means that artificial symmetry, extraneous ornament, and simple mimicry of traditional designs should all be left by the wayside.

Instead, according to this design, the spaces inside determine where the walls on the outside will go and not vice versa. International designers felt that the best way to achieve this was to construct houses with skeletal frames that supported exterior curtain walls. Because these walls weren't load bearing, glazing could, and was, placed just about anywhere. Steel casement windows were sometimes lined up in bold, horizontal banks on one elevation, and then sprinkled individually on another elevation. Corner windows—with plate glass connecting two sides of the house—were standard fare, especially if a great view was available.

Generally, International designs were one- or two-story asymmetrical buildings, with flat roofs and rounded corners. Balconies and steel pipe handrails were common. Glass block was used liberally to let in light, while simultaneously preserving privacy. The exterior surfaces were invariably smooth and devoid of trim. To maintain this appearance, windows were installed flush to the outside surface instead of recessed.

Unfortunately, the International idea that "less is more" never appealed to a large number of American homebuyers, who preferred homes that were warmer and more familiar. However, the International style was, and still continues to be, a very popular design for commercial and industrial buildings.

DESIGNERS OF MODERN HOUSES often think of them as "machines to live in."

MODERN STYLE

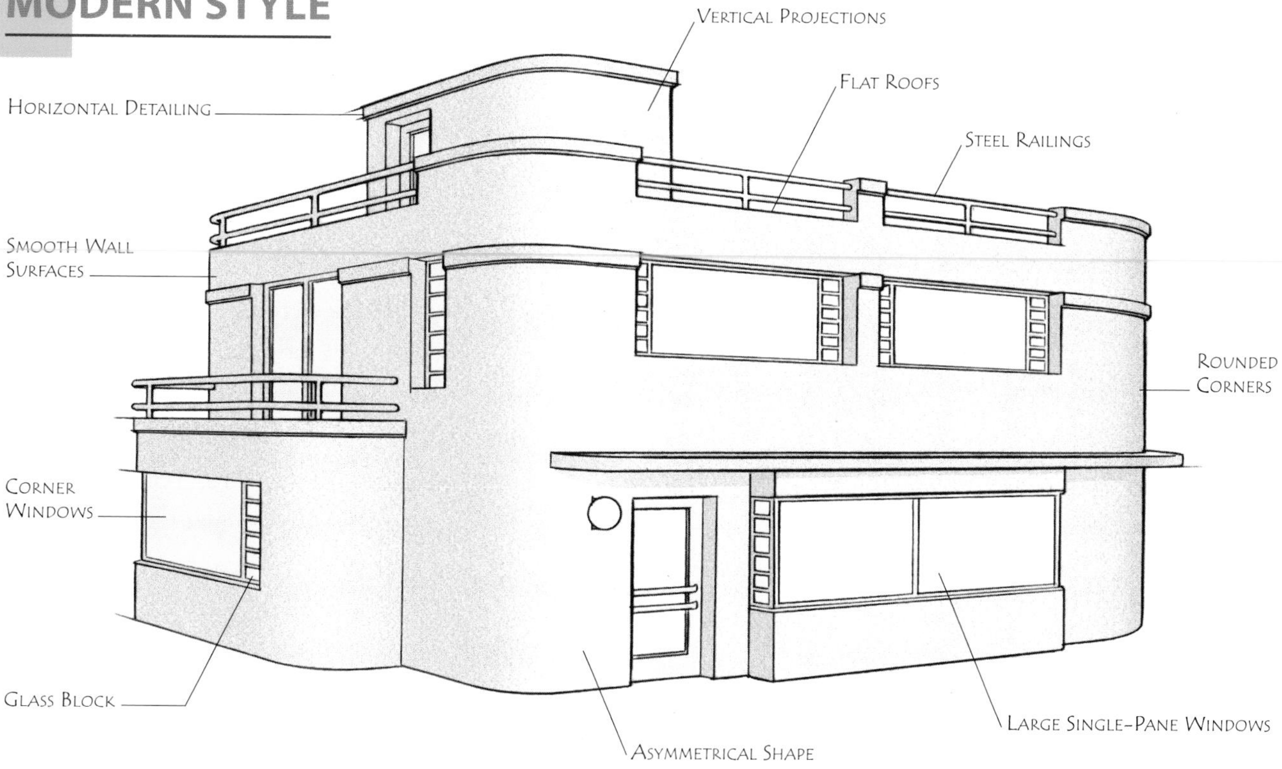

Vertical Projections
Flat Roofs
Steel Railings
Horizontal Detailing
Smooth Wall Surfaces
Rounded Corners
Corner Windows
Glass Block
Asymmetrical Shape
Large Single-Pane Windows

CHAPTER 2

TRIMWORK FOR ROOFS

JUST ABOUT EVERY PIECE OF ROOF TRIM has a bipolar personality. On the one hand, trimwork around the roof area adds distinction. In many of the architectural styles covered in the previous chapter, roof moldings and other trim separate one style from the next. But even though it may appear ornamental, roof trimwork is almost always doing a serious job. The most serious one, of course, is to seal the junction between the roof and the walls so that water from rain and snow can't get inside the building. Another is sealing the house from insects and other wildlife. Attic spaces are perfect nesting spots for bees, birds, and squirrels, and it is much easier to keep them from getting in than it is to get rid of them afterwards. But roof trim isn't all about creating impervious barriers. Many soffits are designed with ventilation in mind. When these vents are combined with other roof vents, the free passage of air keeps the roof framing and sheathing from being damaged by rot.

RAKE TRIM

A RAKE BOARD IS A TRIM PIECE that is installed just below the roofing material on a gable end. For most houses built since World War II, this is a pretty simple treatment: just a single board, usually a 1×8 or 1×10, that covers the end of the roof sheathing. Occasionally, a second board is added, usually a 1×2 or a 1×4, along the top edge of the rake board. This beefs up the trim and creates an appealing shadow line.

On older houses, the rake treatment can be more involved. One common approach is to add a crown molding over a flat rake board just below the roofing. Another is to add an ornately carved cove molding. There is no structural reason to use either of these molding boards. The point is to have the rakes share the same decoration as the other trim boards on the house.

Installing Rakes. Rake boards should be nailed against the wall sheathing and over the end of the roof sheathing. This keeps water from penetrating the edges of the roof plywood, which could lead to plywood delamination. Typically, rake boards are installed before the finished roofing material and the roofing felt; the roofing felt should cover the top of the rake. Drip-edge flashing, sometimes called a rake edge, goes on next.

ELABORATE GABLE-END TRIMWORK, top left, is a common feature on many houses. Here, the rake board combines with large brackets and dentil molding to form a classic design.

A TRIANGULAR RETURN, left, serves as a terminus for a rake where it meets the eaves of the house. Note how the inlaid trim echoes the bracket in the peak of the roof.

This keeps water from getting between the rake and the roofing and running down behind the siding. Once the rake, felt, and flashing are installed, the finished roofing material goes on, usually overhanging the flashing by about ½ inch.

Dealing with Eaves. Where the rake meets the eave wall of the house, the rake must be made wider to completely cover the end of the overhang. There are several ways this can be done, but the most common practice is to cut the rake flush with the adjacent wall overhang, and then use a small triangular block to cover the rest of the overhang. In most cases, the block is nailed into the house wall and the bottom of the rake.

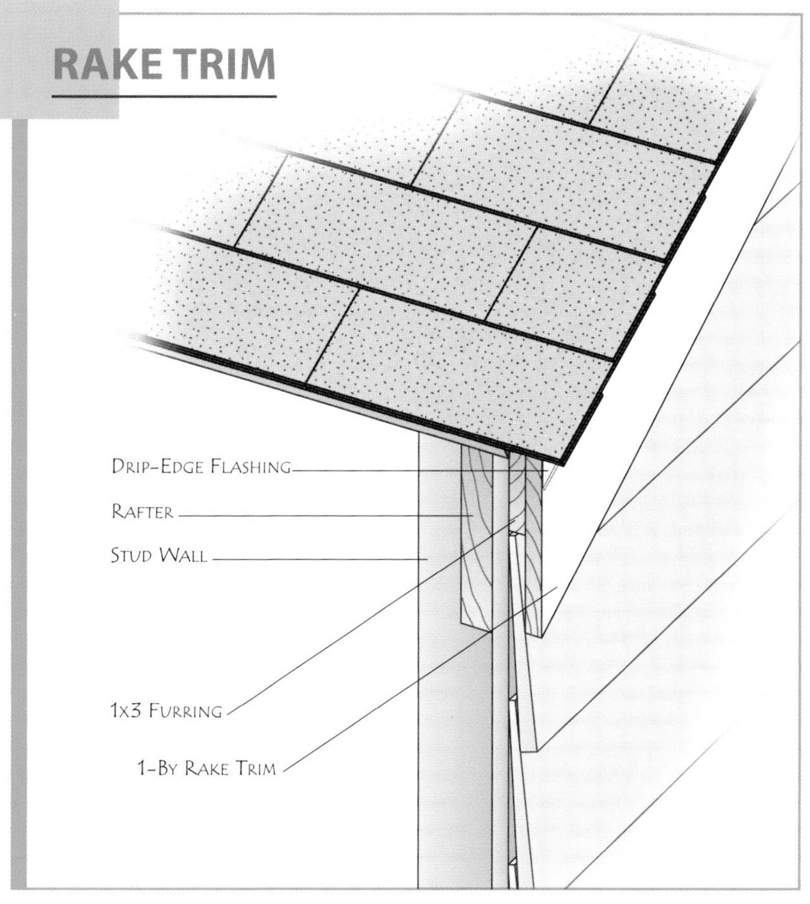

A COMPLEMENTARY PAINT COLOR adds distinction to this simple rake treatment. A built-up rake creates a pleasing texture.

GABLE OVERHANGS

IN MANY CASES, a gable overhang takes the place of the simple rake board. On most newer houses, these box overhangs aren't very big, usually about 6 or 8 inches wide. Because they're so narrow, they don't provide much protection from the sun or the rain. Their purpose is ornamental, either to match trim treatments elsewhere on the house or simply to make the roof deck look thicker and more substantial.

On some houses, particularly sprawling ranch models with a low-pitched roof and wide eave overhangs, gable overhangs can be quite a bit wider—2- and 3-foot-wide versions are not unusual. These wider overhangs can be functional, especially on a single-story house, but generally, they too are ornamental.

Though these two types have similar purposes, they are constructed in completely different ways. The narrow overhang boxes are usually fabricated on the ground and then nailed to the gable ends before these walls are raised. Cantilevered roof sheathing

INSTALLING BRACKETS OF VARIOUS DESIGNS is a popular way to add ornamentation to deep gable overhangs.

SMART TIP WASP PATROL

One of the favorite nesting sights for wasps is under roof overhangs. Like many unsavory members of the animal world, if you don't bother them they probably won't bother you. But if you want to paint the house or do something else where a nest is located, you've got to get rid of the nest.

The best way to do this is with a wasp killer in an aerosol can with a jet spray. These cans can deliver the spray up to 20 feet off the ground. Just wait until dark, when all the wasps are in the nest, and soak the entire nest. If you see wasps around the next day, repeat the procedure.

that extends past the gable end supports the gable box.

Wider Gables. The wider overhangs are more difficult and expensive to build and install because they are heavier and need more support. This support is achieved by installing 2×4 blocking, called lookouts, every 2 feet along the length of the gable rafters. Each lookout requires a clearance notch cut into the gable rafter. The lookouts are then nailed into the box overhangs, the gable rafter notches, and the next rafter in line.

The overhangs are finished up the same way a simple rake board is installed. First, the roof sheathing is nailed in place. Then, the rake is cut to fit and nailed to the outside of the gable overhang so that it covers the end of the roof sheathing. The roofing felt is then installed over the top of the rake and held in place with drip-edge flashing.

GABLE OVERHANG TRIM

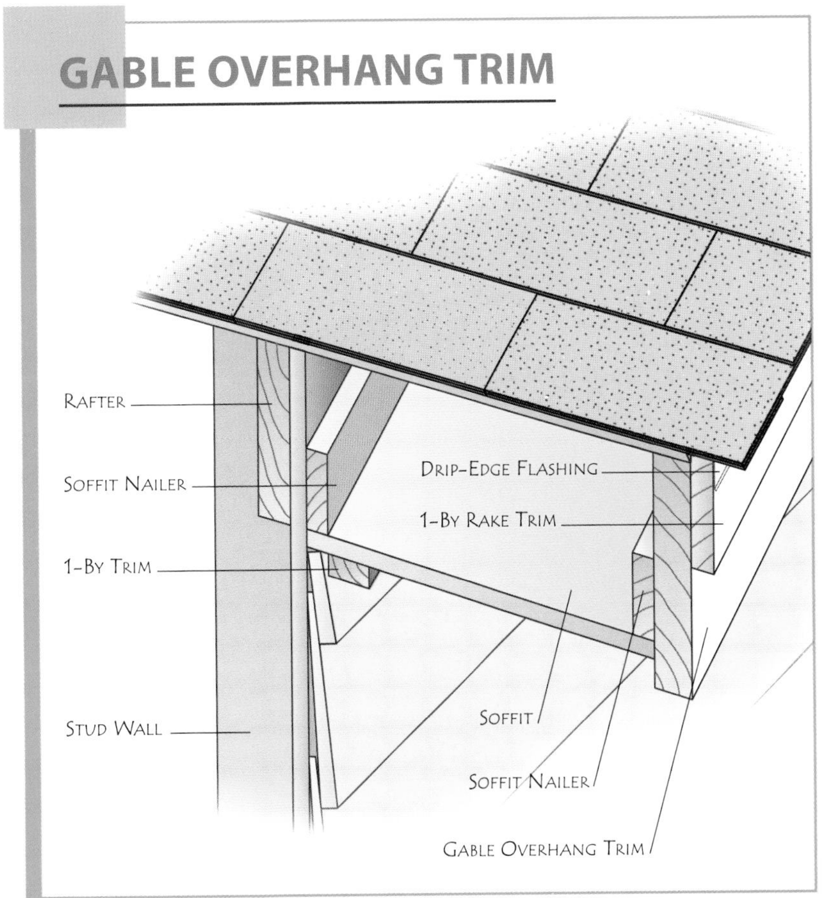

A PROMINENT GABLE, left, adds distinction to this simply designed house. The gable works well with other elements, such as the columns.

ADJOINING GABLES AND GABLE OVERHANGS, above, are unusual and difficult to frame, but they do increase the number of design options on a home.

ORNATE TRIMWORK PATTERNS were often developed on the job site; other patterns could be found in widely circulated pattern books.

Bargeboards

Back in the day, some builders were satisfied with the same simple boxes for gable overhangs that we use today. But many others chose more elaborate presentations. This was especially true in the Gothic Revival era when decoration was considered enviable. For roof trim, their choice for embellishment was the bargeboard—also called a vergeboard or gingerbread—which is nothing more than an ornate rake board, and it's installed the same way.

Bargeboards were cut into many different geometric patterns. Some of these designs were taken from commonly available pattern books. Others were the creations of the local craftsman who was cutting the shapes. These designs also mimicked natural objects such as icicles and snowflakes. Dramatic shapes created dramatic effects, and this type of ornamentation had widespread popularity.

Bargeboard Problems. Unfortunately, wooden gingerbread was not a durable trim item. Ladders would easily break thinner sections, and repeated painting dulled the edges and filled the gaps. This, of course, required more rigorous scraping at repainting time, which in turn caused more breakage of delicate pieces. One-hundred years ago, this trim was difficult to fabricate. But these days, scroll saws and jigsaws make relatively short work of cutting intricate patterns.

Bargeboards rarely appear on the eave side of a roof. They were confined to the gables and stop as soon as they intersected the trim of an adjacent wall. Because bargeboards would hang so low on the gable overhang, the trim elements for the eave overhang were simply cut to abut the back side of the bargeboard, which made a tight transition between two trim surfaces much easier.

Repairing Bargeboard

IF A SECTION OF A BARGEBOARD is broken or missing, often a simple repair can be made without the help of a professional. Start by measuring the void left by the missing section. Then, trace onto heavy paper or cardboard the pattern that is repeated on a part of the bargeboard that is in good shape. Next, transfer the pattern onto a piece of wood that is the same thickness as the existing trim board. Cut the shape with a jigsaw; sand the board smooth; and coat with latex primer. Fit the repaired board into the opening on the overhang, and screw it into place. Finish up with two coats of paint.

MANY BARGEBOARD PATTERNS, left, are based on themes found in nature, such as this climbing vine.

GINGERBREAD TRIM, above, used in moderation makes a bold design statement and can become the focal point of the facade.

FASCIA AND SOFFIT TRIMWORK

JUST ABOUT EVERY ROOF is framed using one of two similar systems. The first, and oldest, features roof rafters. In their basic configuration, these 2×8 or 2×10 boards extend from the top plates of the outside house walls to the ridge at the top of the roof. This arrangement forms two sides of a triangle. The third side is created when the bottoms of the rafters are nailed to ceiling joists in the upstairs rooms of the house.

The second system is also based on a triangle. But this one isn't built in place; it's usually fabricated off site. These assemblies are called trusses, and they are made of 2×4s that are nailed securely together. Trusses feature extra support webbing inside the triangle that works like the cords of a suspension bridge. Because of these supports, smaller boards can carry the same weight that larger rafters do.

Rafters are usually placed 16 inches apart, while trusses usually fall 24 inches apart. In both cases, there are cavities between the framing members that must be enclosed to make a tight house. The most common way to do this is to install a fascia board over the ends of the rafters (or trusses). Then, nail soffit material underneath the rafter tails (or truss ends). This simple approach creates a box overhang that keeps water and animals out.

ORNATE SOFFITS AND FASCIA are popular design elements for many Victorian homes. Note the distinctive corner treatment at left.

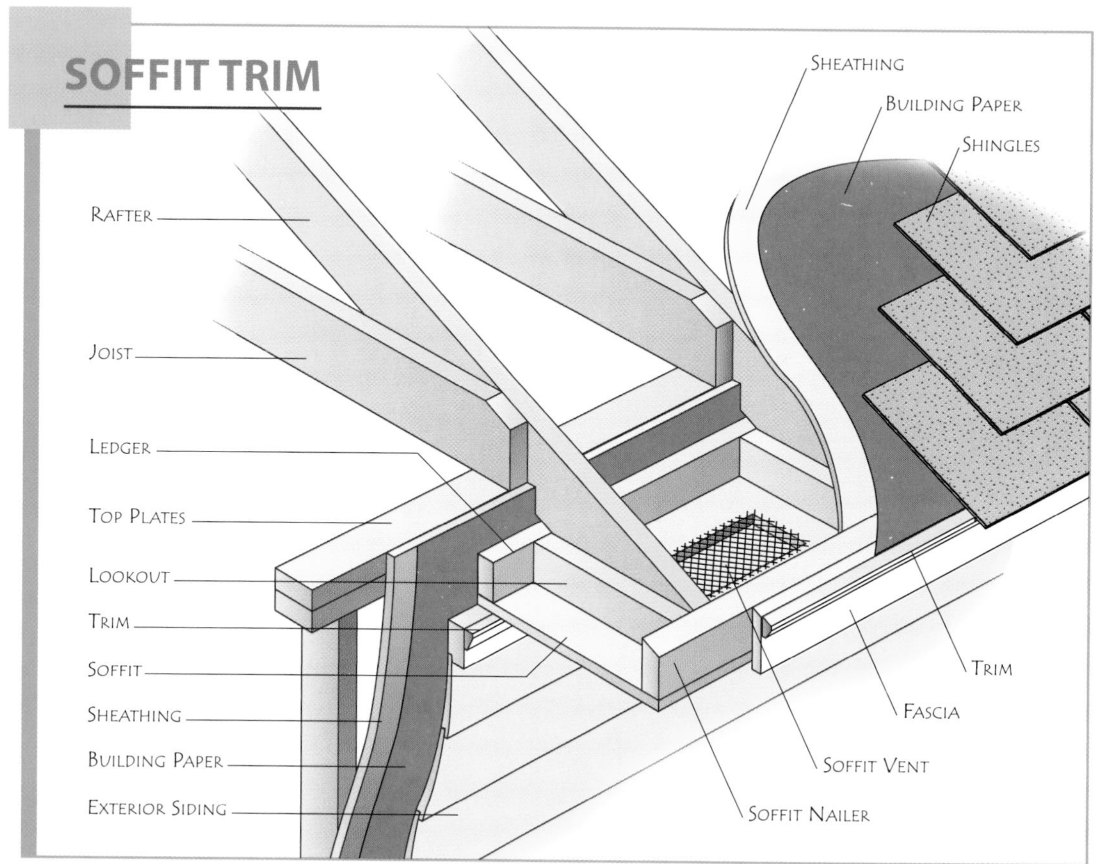

THIS MODERN INTERPRETATION OF AN EAVE, opposite top, features evenly spaced brackets supporting a standing-seam metal roof.

WIDE OVERHANGS, opposite bottom, provide shade for windows and doors. Note how the porch ceiling matches the finish treatment of the soffits.

Most eave overhangs are pretty simple, just unadorned boxes 8 to 12 inches wide. Sometimes, classic ranch houses and Arts and Crafts designs feature overhangs that are a good bit wider, up to 2 or 3 feet. But even these provide little or no decoration. In the past, eave overhangs were often highly decorated. On Italianate houses in particular, wide overhangs featured large sculptural brackets, sometimes installed in pairs, that made the roof look substantial and indestructible.

DORMERS

DORMERS CAN BE AS PLAIN OR AS ORNATE, above, as the rest of the trimwork on the house.

DORMERS ADD LIGHT AND PROVIDE VENTILATION, below, but they also break up large expanses of roof that would overwhelm the facade of the house.

STRICTLY SPEAKING, dormers are not trimwork. They are structural roof components designed to make better use of the attic space under the rafters. Without the light and view they provide, few people would find such space habitable. But from a design perspective, dormers act as roof embellishments and visually break up big expanses of dull roofing.

Dormers are almost always found on steep roofs; shallow-pitched roofs don't have enough headroom under the rafters to make the space usable. They have been successfully used on everything from early colonial shelters to present-day McMansions.

Trim Treatments. Though exceptions do exist, dormers have usually been trimmed in the same way as other components of the house. For example, a bargeboard on the main roof gable would be duplicated on the dormer gable—albeit in a smaller scale so it looks appropriate for the size of the dormer. As a dormer increases in size, less modification in the scale is required. A full shed dormer, for instance, usually features the same type and size of trim that's used elsewhere on the house.

There's no question that repairing or maintaining dormer trim is a nuisance and can be dangerous. Some trim is accessible from the window, but the bulk of it must be dealt with from the roof, and a steep roof at that. Many homeowners feel perfectly comfortable doing other chores around the house, but working on a steep roof is only for experienced contractors who have valid insurance policies.

SMART TIP BACK PRIMING

Because dormers are so hard to work on, it's a good idea to minimize their problems. One small way to do this, whether you do your own work or hire someone, is to make sure that every board that's replaced is properly primed. Each board should be back-primed—all six sides covered with primer. Except for extreme water exposure, nothing makes a coat of paint fail as quickly as a bad priming job.

TIE DORMERS TO THE REST OF THE FACADE by duplicating design elements from other parts of the house, such as trimwork, window and siding styles, and paint colors.

CUPOLAS

FOR HUNDREDS OF YEARS, ridge-mounted cupolas have provided great ventilation for house attics. Some of these structures were completely open to the air, but most had louvered sides that let air pass through and kept the rain and snow out. Cupolas worked in the same way that chimneys do: as low-pressure wind or breeze moves over the top of the cupola or chimney, it draws out high-pressure air from inside the house. Keeping air moving through a building is the easiest way to reduce or eliminate damage caused by rot.

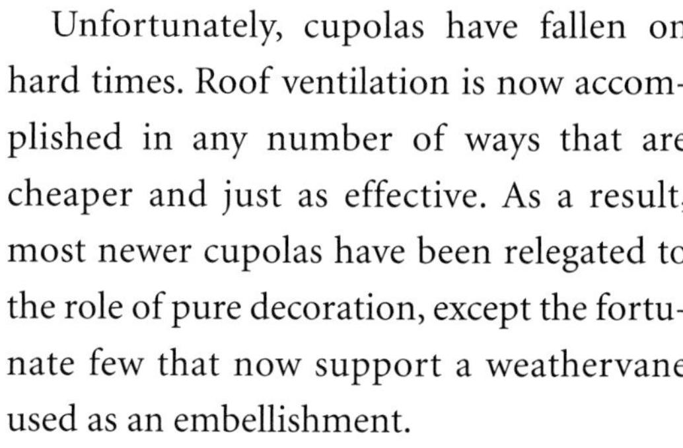

Unfortunately, cupolas have fallen on hard times. Roof ventilation is now accomplished in any number of ways that are cheaper and just as effective. As a result, most newer cupolas have been relegated to the role of pure decoration, except the fortunate few that now support a weathervane used as an embellishment.

Because old cupolas covered a hole in the roof, the base of the cupola had to be flashed to the roof to prevent water leaks. But most of today's cupolas don't even break through the roofing. Instead they just sit on the shingles and are attached with simple roof-mounted brackets. One of these basic 20-inch-square cupolas is available at home centers for under $100.

Cupola Trim. Like dormers that were discussed earlier, the trim on cupolas usually matches the trim on the house. In older houses, this can be pretty elaborate. But on contemporary houses a cupola is reduced to a simple square box with a small hip roof on the top. The sides of the structure are usually painted to match the house, and the roof is covered with the same shingles used on the roof of the house.

IN THE PAST, CUPOLAS, above, provided ventilation for attics. Today, many cupolas are used for ornamentation only and are simply mounted on the ridge of the roof.

CUPOLA TRIM OFTEN matches the rest of the house. But adding a cupola creates an opportunity to include an unexpected design accent, such as the copper roof on the cupola shown **left.**

LARGER THAN THE TYPICAL CUPOLA, this structure, **opposite,** allows light into the rooms below. Note how the porch shades the first-floor rooms from direct sunlight.

Instant Cupola

ROOFS may be ventilated with cupolas—small structures on the roof with louvered sides to allow for airflow and a shingled roof to keep out the weather. Some companies sell ready-to-assemble cupolas, or you can design and make your own.

A typical cupola has four side panels, consisting of two miter-cut 2x4 corner boards and 1x2 louvers glued into routed mortises in the corner boards. Louvers should be spaced close enough together to block light when viewed straight on.

To mount a cupola, cut a hole in the roof and join the two structures with framing hardware. Add the necessary flashing to close the seams between the cupola and the shingles. When installed, you can staple screening to the back of the side pieces to keep insects from entering.

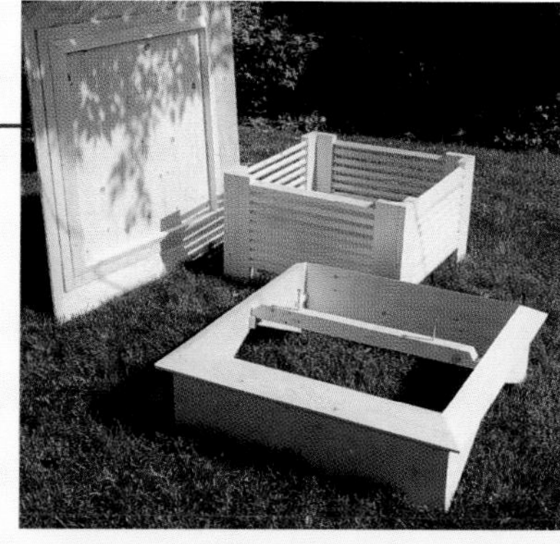

READY-MADE CUPOLAS in kit form are available through many specialty and lumber supply stores.

A CUPOLA can be used to ventilate a building, or it can be installed as a purely decorative element.

ROOF-VENTING TRIM

A ROOF HAS TO BREATHE, which means that it has to allow air to pass through the attic and under the roof sheathing to keep the sheathing and the framing members from rotting. Without this air movement, condensation alone could cause serious damage. In the old days, house construction was much looser than it is today. As a result, more air could move through the structure and keep everything reasonably dry. As soon as houses started to tighten up, they started to have trouble. When fastidious use of caulk, vapor barriers, and insulation became the fashions of the day, people began to understand that tighter is not always better.

Decorative Venting. The only trim components that regularly involve ventilation are gable vents and soffit vents. Gable vents come in round, triangular, and rectangular units that are made of aluminum, wood, or plastic. These vents are installed in the gable ends, just below the roof ridge. Air moving across one vent will pull air from the attic. The air that leaves is replaced with new air coming in through the vent on the opposite gable end. You can either paint a gable vent to blend in with the house's siding or make it stand out as a decorative element.

As mentioned earlier, in an old house gable vents usually provide enough ventilation. But in newer, tight houses, soffit ventilation is also required. Soffit vents are installed in the eave overhangs and allow air to wash under the sheathing. These vents have to be used in conjunction with other vents, such as gable, roof, or continuous ridge vents, or they won't work.

SMART TIP ADDING SOFFIT VENTS

If you don't have soffit vents in your house and have noticed some mildew in the attic, you should consider adding some vents to improve attic air circulation. The easiest ones to install are the 2-inch-diameter models or strip vents shown here. Begin by marking the middle of the space between the rafters or trusses. Remember, rafters are usually spaced 16 inches apart while trusses are 24 inches apart. Then, cut the hole in the soffit; remove the waste; and push or screw the vent into place. Soffit vents are usually used in conjunction with ridge vents.

There are two common types of soffit vents. One is a piece of continuous, louvered, aluminum venting. This material is about 2 inches wide and 8 to 10 feet long, and it is installed down the middle of the soffit, usually with a narrow board on each side. The other type is a small (usually about 2 inches in diameter) round, louvered aluminum plug that is installed in holes drilled into the soffit boards. These round models are generally the choice for a remodeling job in which venting is needed but tearing apart the whole soffit is not an option.

ROUND OR SQUARE GABLE VENTS, opposite top, were the only choice in attic ventilation for many years. Their design often provided an accent to blank walls.

CONTINUOUS SOFFIT VENTS, opposite bottom, are the best choice for many modern designs. In these cases, the vents do not serve as a design accent but to provide ventilation only.

LARGE LOUVERED VENTS, right, provide a steady flow of fresh air to the attic space of this garage. These vents match others on this large shingle-style house.

CHAPTER 3

ENTRY DETAILS

IN THE OLD DAYS, the front door was very important because it was the only way in and out for people and everything else, including light. These days (think the suburbs, where every house has an attached garage) the front door has become vestigial: the family uses the garage door or the back door. The front door is forced into action only on Halloween.

We may not use the front door much anymore, but that doesn't mean it isn't still important. In most houses, it remains the focal point of the front elevation, the natural resting spot for roving eyes. And for hundreds of years, front doors have been the battlefield on which different styles and fashions have fought. Colonial designers may have loved the simplicity of a basic, unadorned entry. But the Victorians thought it was the perfect place to exercise some serious decoration—to say nothing of a starting point for porticoes, pergolas, and porte cocheres.

DOORS & CASINGS

EXCEPT FOR RELATIVELY SHORT PERIODS when double entry doors were popular, the single front door has been the default choice for American residential buildings. It is, after all, a good way to get inside. It's simple and easy to operate, and it has only a few moving parts that are very long lasting. But just because it's simple doesn't mean it can't get dressed up and go to the ball.

The first ornamentation involved is the door itself. In early colonial days, just a few slabs of wood nailed together would do the trick. But soon flat- or raised-panel doors predominated (and still do today, with the ubiquitous six-panel steel entry door). The next change was replacing some of the wood panels with glass. Plain glass, of course, was the most common. But in more expensive houses, beveled, leaded, etched, and stained glass appeared. All were a good way to let in more light and give the door more design texture.

THE SHAPE OF THE CURVED-TOP DOOR is echoed in the door surround, creating a focal point for the front facade.

LOCKED UP

Replacing locksets and adding a dead bolt to your front door are two common home improvement jobs that are well within the abilities of most homeowners. Both pieces of hardware come with easy-to-follow instructions. The only trick is to make sure you buy the right size hardware for your door. Locksets and dead bolts are sized to the thickness of the door. So measure your door before you go shopping. The lockset packaging will list the door sizes that the lock fits.

MANY EARLY HOUSE STYLES, above left, relied on plain door casing. These wide trim boards seem to support the unusual head casing. The small glass panels would give way to larger areas of glass around doors in later designs.

PAINTING DOOR CASING A CONTRASTING COLOR, above, is a good way to draw attention to the entry.

Front Door Options

DOORS COME IN A VARIETY of styles and designs. In addition to the traditional wood doors, manufacturers now offer doors made of steel and fiberglass. These newer materials resist shrinking, swelling, and warping. They both stand up to extremes in weather. Some fiberglass doors contain a faux-wood grain molded into their finish. Both steel and fiberglass can be painted or stained to look like wood.

ALTHOUGH THEY LOOK LIKE WOOD, many exterior doors are made of fiberglass, **opposite,** or steel, **above.** In either case, buyers have the option of selecting from factory-finished doors or using finishing kits supplied by the manufacturer. Many manufacturers offer snap-in casing for their doors, **above right.** You can create your own entry design by mixing components, such as sidelights, glass patterns, transoms, and distinctive trimwork, **right.**

Door Accessories. Adding elaborate hardware is another decorative approach. Heavy brass door knockers, mail slots, hinges, and latch sets all draw attention to the door—as do oversized address numbers, distinctive light fixtures, and, more recently, landscape lighting that brightens everyone's way home.

The decoration may vary but the construction doesn't. All doors are mounted in jambs that are joined with nails or screws to the house framing. These jambs are decorated with casing boards, both inside and out, that help support the jam. No matter how plain the overall trim treatment may be, the outside door casings are almost always more ornate than other trim boards. Fluted or beaded side casings are common. Columns right next to the jambs give the impression of supporting a heavy beam above the door.

ENTRY-WALL CONSTRUCTION

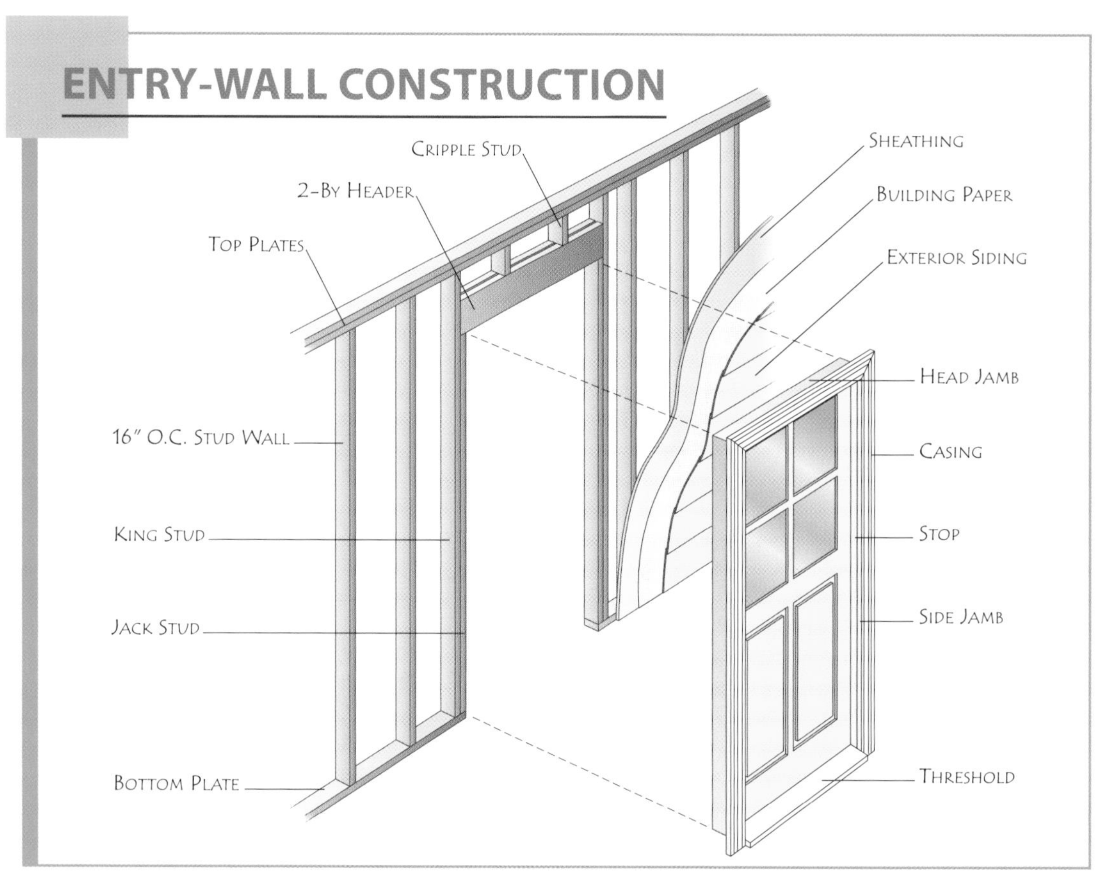

DECORATIVE LIGHTING AND BRASS HARDWARE, above left, help draw attention to this simply designed entry.

HOUSES IN THE MODERN STYLE, opposite top, must rely on a strong door design for entry ornamentation.

DOUBLE DOORS, opposite bottom, look best when used as part of a large entry area, such as the one shown here.

Screen Doors

ALTHOUGH MOST FORMAL ENTRIES do not include a screen door, there is something very welcoming about an old-fashioned wooden screen door. They work best on country-style houses and houses designed for a warm-weather climate, and they are the only option if the porch is screened in.

NEVER-FAIL WELCOMING DETAILS, opposite, include a wide, shady porch and a simple screen door. In areas of the country subject to harsh summer temperatures, a screened-in porch, **above,** is the only way to enjoy the outdoors. The screen door shown **right** complements the formal entry. Create a focal point by using a bright color on your screen door, **far right.**

PEDIMENTS AND HEAD CASINGS

DOOR TRIM CAN BE PRETTY SEDATE, just some painted 1×4 pine or 2-inch-wide brick mold on the side and top jambs. This treatment often works well for contemporary houses, but it's never been a common feature of older house styles. In the past, the entry door was always the focal point of the front elevation and was decorated accordingly.

Enhancing the Trim. In most cases, designers and builders have a basic choice to make: do they want a flat head casing with a drip cap on top, or a more ornate pediment? And if they choose a pediment, should it be full or split? Their next decision is how much this piece of trim should be embellished. Pediments, for example, can be pretty

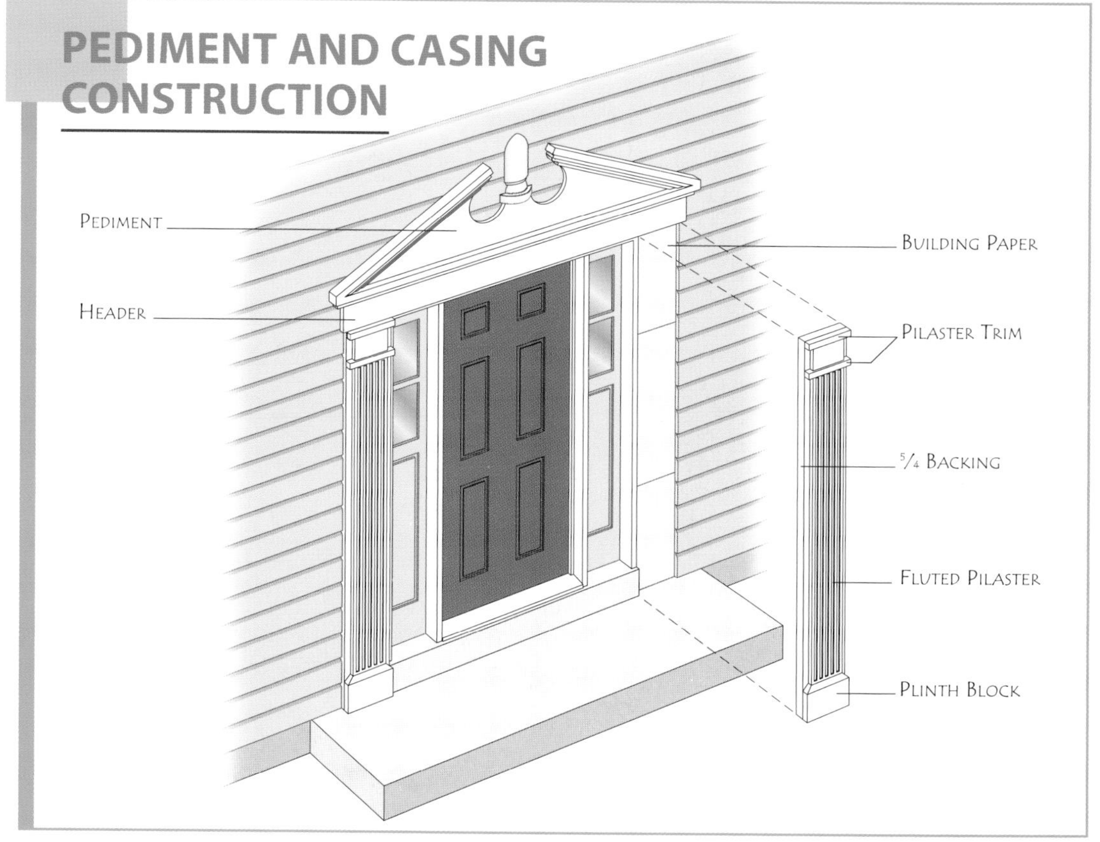

A BUILT-UP HEAD CASING, above, enlivens the entry to this house. Note how the head casing design is carried over to the nearby windows.

GRAND ENTRANCES, above right, call for grand trimwork treatments. This entry design contains a number of classic molding types, including dentil molding and pilasters.

straightforward, just a shallow triangle installed so that it slightly projects from the siding. And, of course, they can be much more ornate. Hand-carved split pediments are common in the older house styles. And the more expensive the house, the more eye-catching was the pediment.

Plainer styles, such as Federal and Colonial Revival, lean toward plainer head casings. A simple horizontal piece the same width and thickness as the side casings is a common solution. But usually it is a thicker and wider board, sometimes with a crown or cove molding installed along its top edge.

Typically, the amount of decoration used on the front door is greatly reduced on other entry doors at the side or back of the house. This approach certainly reduces costs a bit. More importantly, the trim makes a clear design statement: the front door is the proper entry of the house and the others are merely portals of convenience.

HERE'S AN EXCEPTION TO THE RULE of using sedate trimwork on secondary entries. This patio entrance gets the full trimwork treatment.

SMART TIP SAFE SECURITY

Sidelights give much light without sacrificing much security. But they do sacrifice some because an intruder could quickly break one pane, reach in, turn the lock button, open the door from the outside, and walk in. One way around this is to install a dead bolt that has a keyed cylinder on the inside. Without the key it won't open even when the sidelight is broken. Just be sure to keep the key close by and in plain view. In case of a fire you may not have time to look around for it.

EVEN SIMPLY DESIGNED SIDELIGHTS, below, seem to expand the size of the entry. Sidelights allow light into the house without sacrificing security.

IF PRIVACY IS A CONCERN, opposite, consider using stained- or etched-glass sidelights. They allow light to pass through and add style while maintaining privacy.

ADDING GLASS

One of the reasons that doors aren't windows is that we all want a little security. After all, windows are easy to break and doors aren't. For protection, a big heavy door with a strong lock and no glass around it would make for the most secure door. Unfortunately, this door also makes for a very dark foyer and no easy way to see the visitor on the other side, which has always been a dilemma. How much security do you give up to get the convenience of some glass?

Sidelights

Sidelights are a pretty good compromise. Usually just 6 inches wide, they don't provide access even when broken. But they do let in plenty of light and make it easy to see who is at your door. Some sidelights are operable, but most are fixed. Some are half as high as the door, but most are the same height. Sidelights also visually expand the door, making it look more substantial from the outside and ultimately more inviting.

In the past, these units were installed separately, like windows, and then the door was fitted between. But these days, the sidelights and door are one assembly that goes into a single rough opening. One of the biggest advantages of this type of construction is that it allows the sill (usually aluminum clad) to extend without a break from side jamb to side jamb. This reduces the chance of leaks in one of the more leak-prone areas of a house. This assembly approach also lets consumers pick any number of different combinations of doors, sidelights, and transom windows to fit their design requirements.

SMART TIP A DRAFT PROPOSAL

Older decorative windows, like some of the ones shown here, can be drafty. If the problem exists where the window meets the window frame, caulk can fill the crack. But drafts can also come through old glazing compound on transom windows and the lead on leaded and stained-glass windows. You can easily replace the compound on a transom unit. But working on leaded glass of any type is more difficult. In most cases, these repairs are better left to a professional. You can also tighten things up by installing plastic storm windows over the drafty units.

THE TRANSOM WINDOW ABOVE THIS SIMPLE DOOR, above, enhances the overall design and places the top of the door trim in line with the window trim on the first floor.

ONE WAY TO UNIFY AN ENTRY DESIGN is to use the same type of glazing in both the transom and sidelights, **right.**

Transom Windows

A step up from the plain head casings and ornate pediments, discussed in the previous section, is the use of glass above an entry door. The most common choices are multipane transom, fanlight, and Palladian windows. In colonial times, when glass was imported, this was an expensive decoration. But as more glass was made in America, the price came down and the use went up.

Transom, fanlight, and Palladian windows are very similar to sidelights, except that the former have one big leg up: they let in plenty of light but don't compromise security at all. While it's common to see one of these windows used by itself, they are usually installed over doorways that have sidelights. This arrangement creates an oversized entry with real design substance.

Choosing Transom Windows. The size of the panes in transom lights usually match the panes in the sidelights, and the whole window stretches from sidelight jamb to sidelight jamb. Palladian windows, on the other hand, are no wider than the door. Fanlight windows are used both ways.

While some transom windows are operable for ventilation purposes, most are fixed to eliminate rain and snow penetration. The same is true for fanlights and Palladian windows. Transom windows are reserved for use above doors, but the curved shapes of the fanlight and Palladian units are often echoed on windows elsewhere on the facade. All three kinds are generally glazed with common flat glass, but you can also choose from among beveled, leaded, and stained glass.

A FANLIGHT WINDOW, below left, complements this classic front entry that includes fluted pilasters and an ornamental keystone in the head casing.

AN OLD IDEA IS GIVEN A NEW TWIST, below, in this entry design. Colonial designers often used small panes of glass out of necessity. Here small panes add distinction to a contemporary home.

PORTICOES

AS AN ENTRY EMBELLISHMENT, a portico isn't subtle. Consisting of a pediment or gable roof supported by massive columns, a portico leaves no doubt of the location of the proper entry. A typical example covers most or all of the front elevation and is usually two stories high. Sometimes it also extends down both sides of the house or connects the house to an outbuilding by means of a colonnade (columned walkway).

Because such a major structure has always been expensive, porticoes are usually reserved for more prestigious houses. For many years, they were practically required on large public buildings such as banks and government offices. Typically, the columns are made of wood or limestone and are difficult to build, install, and maintain. The rest of the structure has problems, too. The relatively simple task of painting a porch ceiling, for example, becomes a major project when the ceiling is inside a two-story portico.

THE TEXTBOOK EXAMPLE OF A PORTICO, above, features a pediment supported by columns, creating a grand entry.

ALTHOUGH IT BENDS THE RULES, as most modern homes do, the house shown **below** displays some of the characteristics of a classic portico.

SMART TIP COLUMN BASE DECAY

If you are lucky enough to have stone columns on your house, you don't have to worry about rot. But most residential columns are wood and are prone to rot where the column meets its base. An experienced contractor should check severe damage. But shallow rot can be repaired with epoxy wood fillers. These two-part formulations are waterproof, so repairs made with them won't be subject to more water damage.

THE ENTRY OVERHANG of this house mimics the trim details used on the upper-story eaves. This entry combines classic and modern elements.

These structures may seem a bit over the top and harder to maintain than most would want, but from a design standpoint they are purely remarkable. Depending on the architect's loyalty to tradition, each column can be an architecture primer on Greek and Roman building practices. The classical design orders stipulated the size, proportion, and shape of the columns and the roof elements above.

NOW FOR SOMETHING COMPLETELY DIFFERENT, left, this modern house has a hint of a portico over the main entry.

PORTICO DESIGN SHOULD FOLLOW THE DESIGN OF THE HOUSE as shown **opposite left,** where the columns, roof pitch, balustrade, and accessories all match elements found on other parts of this Victorian-style house.

THE PORTICO REINTERPRETED could be the title of the design shown **opposite right.** Its lines and shapes are contemporary, but its intent in that of a classic portico.

Outer Doors

BECAUSE MOST FRONT DOORS are rarely used these days, there's not much reason to install an outer or storm door over them. But for other entry doors, or if your front door does serve as a main entry, storm doors are convenient and easy to install. Once you get the door home, it should take only a few hours to get the job done. Just don't assume that the aluminum storm door selection at your local home center is all that's available. Wood doors with interchangeable screen and glass panels are still made and are very good choices for older houses. They do increase the energy efficiency of the entry, and during nice weather, you can leave the main door open and enjoy the views and fresh air through the storm door.

The reason that so many older porticoes look the same is because so many designers tried to follow these classical rules as they were interpreted in the pattern books of the day.

A Twist on the Classical. To a purist, a portico may have a specific definition, but in reality any covered entry is called a portico. Many American housing styles make use of a column-supported covered entry.

In the south, especially along the Gulf costs, door-size louvered shutters often served as outer doors. Louvered panels allow fresh air in while keeping harsh sunlight out. These types of outer doors were often installed with double inner doors.

OUTER DOORS INCREASE ENERGY EFFICIENCY, allow you to enjoy the views while keeping the door closed, and protect the main door from the elements. Most models, **opposite,** contain glass panels. Louvered models, **right,** complement Southern-style architecture.

PERGOLAS

ADDING A PERGOLA is another common way that designers use to dress up an entryway. A pergola is an open structure that is usually 8 to 10 feet high and consists of joists, supported by a couple of beams, which are supported by posts held in the ground. Usually the ends of the joists and beams are carved into a decorative profile to provide some texture for the whole structure. Pergolas have never been very expensive to build, as they have no roofs, no walls, and no continuous foundations.

Pergolas can be used like arbors to support spreading vines. Once this vegetation fills in between the joists, it blocks the sun and provides a wonderful, shady retreat. But even without vines, a pergola provides plenty of shade in the morning and afternoon, when the sun is lower and is blocked by the sides of the joists. During the middle of the day, of course, the sun is too high and the light passes directly between the joists.

Pergolas are usually thought of as private retreats and therefore are often built next to a rear door or over a patio. Narrow versions are also used to connect the rear entry with outbuildings such as garages and garden sheds. When used this way, a pergola is like a garden colonnade, without the columns and roof.

Of course, the use of pergolas is not restricted to the back or side entries to the house. Plenty of these structures are built on the front facade, too. They were particularly common on Craftsman houses, where they could visually expand a small front porch or provide some shelter from the front door to a side driveway.

THIS GABLE-STYLE PERGOLA, **above,** shades a second-level deck, which in turn provides protection for the front entry.

PEAKED PERGOLAS, **right,** provide shade and architectural interest for the patio area around a swimming pool.

SMART TIP NO-MAINTENANCE PERGOLAS

If you want to build a pergola yourself—especially one that's going to be covered with a large vine—consider using vinyl components. They won't split, crack, or rot, and you'll never have to paint them, which is a tough job once the vine is filled out. Small pergola kits are available at home centers, and you can order bigger ones form Internet sites such as backyardamerica.com.

LOOKING ALMOST LIKE A TEMPLE, this pergola has both modern and classic design elements. Note the elaborate cornice.

PORTE COCHERES

YOUR CAR IS READY, MADAM. Here is a porte cochere off a side entrance, **above.**

THE DESIGN OF THE PORTE COCHERE, below, extends the look of the main house.

A PORTE COCHERE IS A STRUCTURE that extends from over a doorway (usually the front door) to cover a section of the driveway. The idea is to provide shelter alongside the house for both the car and the people going back and forth. In the days when garages were built separate from the house, a porte cochere made good sense. But as soon as garages started being attached to (or became part of) the house, the need for a porte cochere largely disappeared.

Though frequently beautiful, these structures are expensive to build because a substantial roof has to be carried all the way from the front door over the driveway. This requires more effort and money than required for most full-width front porches. But the convenience of this investment is unmistakable. It's like having a garage right next to the house without the fumes that most attached garages let into the home.

Porte cocheres are usually built using the design vocabulary of front porches. If the house style calls for round tapered columns, that's what is used on the porte cochere. The same is true of the frieze, fascia, any dentils, and the ceiling underneath the roof. Sometimes a porte cochere doesn't tie in directly with the front door. Instead, it's built farther down one side of the house and attached to a section of a wraparound front porch or to a stand-alone side porch that covers a side entry.

Other Entries

WHILE THE FRONT ENTRY usually receives most of the design emphasis, other doors can be important also, especially if they are visible from the street or a neighbor's yard. In most cases, back and side entries tend to be treated less formally, although it makes design sense to use the same materials and types of ornamentation on all parts of the house.

SECONDARY ENTRIES are often treated less formally than the main entry of the house. However, good design calls for an integrated approach to materials and looks throughout the house. Sweeping stairs lead to a covered porch, **below.** Simple trim frames a Dutch door on this back porch, **right.** An angled entry becomes the focal point of this yard, **below right.**

CHAPTER 4

WINDOW & WALL TRIM

HAVING WINDOWS is like having a group of plasma TVs spread throughout your house, each tuned to a different channel. You can check on the weather, the kids, the pets, and the neighbors, all without leaving the kitchen counter or living room sofa. They may let too much heat slip through during the winter. But who wants to live in a dark box when it's cold outside?

Windows are always the focal point of the rooms they brighten. And they play an important design role on the outside of the house. Perfectly aligned double-hung models, all the same size, convey a sense of quiet order; a gaggle of bays, bows, transoms, and casements practically defines architectural exuberance. But as compelling as windows are, many other trim components also adorn the outside walls of a house, including corner boards, friezes, water tables, and pilasters.

WINDOW CASINGS

WINDOW CASINGS are usually more modest than door casings, but the two share basic design features. For example, if an entry door features a head casing pediment, then the window casings, at least on the first floor, will often have similar pediments, albeit usually smaller ones. Sometimes, however, the difference between door and window trim treatments is stark. Early designs, such as Georgian and Federal, had very plain window trim compared to the entry door trim, which was often the most elaborate decoration on the whole building.

Wood window casings are easy to install. After the window is placed in the rough wall opening, the casing boards are nailed to the

ON BRICK HOMES, below, masons can add ornamentation around windows without changing materials.

CONTEMPORARY HOUSES, right, usually rely on simple window casings. Ornate trimwork would look out of place with these large panes of glass.

OLDER HOUSES, opposite, generally feature ornate window treatments.

window jambs and to the wall sheathing and studs that define the rough opening. Except for exposure to weather, these boards function the same way as interior casing trim boards. Because the siding abuts these casing boards, the caulk joint between the siding and trim must be well maintained to keep water from penetrating into the building.

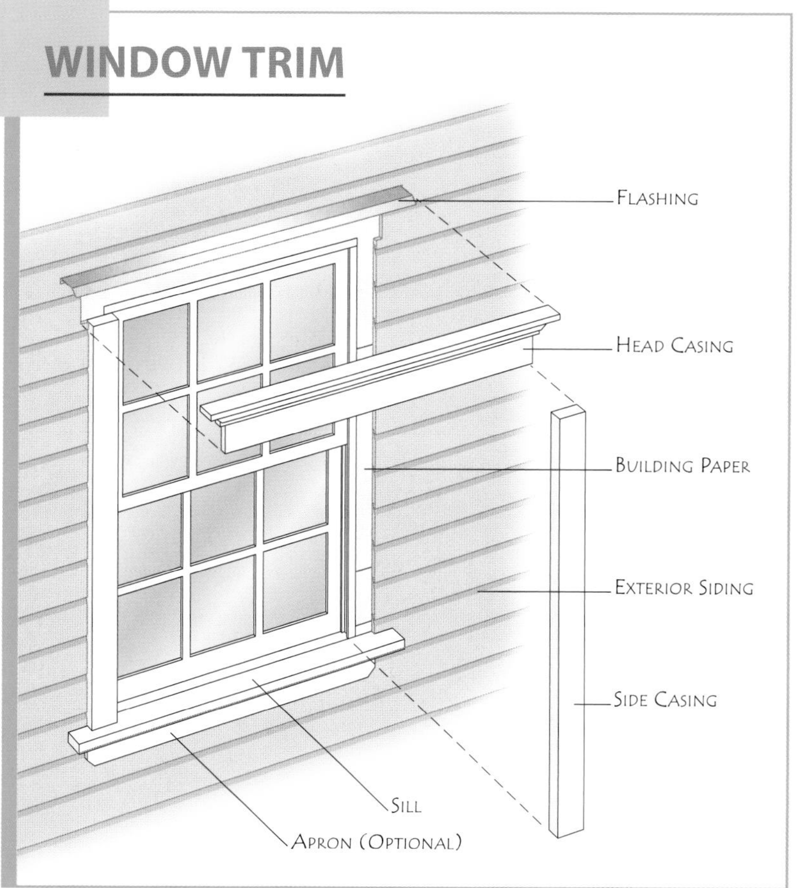

SMART TIP SEASONAL MAINTENANCE CHECK

On old windows that don't have drip caps, the caulk joint between the head casing and the course of siding that rests on it must be maintained. It is a good idea to check this joint every spring and fall. If this caulk is cracked or missing, it needs repair. A quick fix is to recaulk the entire joint. Start by scraping out all the old dry caulk and brushing the space clean of dust and other debris. Then fill the joint completely with silicone caulk.

NOT ALL TRIMWORK is made of wood, **below left,** as shown by the metalwork on this stucco house.

A BRIGHT COLOR PALETTE, below right, helps the trimwork on this window blend with the frieze and brackets above.

Drip Caps. The area that is most vulnerable to moisture penetration is where the siding meets the head casing. The rainwater that flows down the wall is interrupted by this board and splashes in every direction. Though caulk could protect this joint, the better choice has always been to install a drip cap over the head casing to direct water away from the top of the window. These days a drip cap is either built right into the window assembly or it's a separate piece of aluminum.

Traditional drip caps, however, are made of wood and usually project about 1 inch beyond the front edge of the head casing when installed. Often, these caps have a more substantial overhang, especially if this wide projection is part of a more elaborate overall trim treatment. For example, if the head casing features a crown molding along its top edge, the drip cap needs to be wide enough to protect both the casing and the crown.

WINDOW-SIZE ROOFS with open rafters, **above,** offer a unique form of ornamentation.

VICTORIAN-ERA HOUSES, below, often incorporate elaborate window trim painted with bold colors.

TO BE ARCHITECTURALLY CORRECT, even ornamental shutters should look as though they would cover the window when closed, as shown at **right.**

SHUTTER HARDWARE, such as the hinges shown **opposite top,** are one way to tell if the shutters are authentic or merely decoration.

PAINTING SHUTTERS a contrasting color, **opposite bottom,** helps them stand out and complement the exterior color scheme.

SHUTTERS

BEFORE GLASS BECAME AVAILABLE FOR WINDOWS, early versions of shutters were used to cover windows. At night or during storms, they were closed for security and protection. During the day, when the weather was good, they were opened for ventilation and light. After window glass became commonplace, shutters still provided protection and security, albeit on an intermittent basis. During heavy storms, they could be closed to prevent damage to the window glass. And if the house was ever left unoccupied, the shutters could be locked to keep intruders out.

These days, most traditional shutters are ornamental. Even though they may be operable, they aren't used. And most shutters on new houses aren't operable at all. They're usually fiberglass units that are screwed to the siding. Sometimes the use of these fiberglass products is somewhat illogical: if the fenestration (window placement) is such that there's no room for shutters between windows, putting shutters only on the windows where they fit looks silly.

Shutter Hardware. Imitation shutters are a relatively recent introduction. On houses older than sixty or seventy years, the shutters are probably real, which means that they will cover the window openings when closed and are outfitted with the proper hardware. The traditional hardware includes two hinges on the back of each shutter and two pintels mounted in the siding behind each shutter. The hinges sit on the pintels and pivot open and closed. The shutters are held open with shutter dogs and held closed with a lock mechanism.

There are three basic shutter designs: solid, louvered, and a combination of the two. Because modern-day shutters don't do much, the choice is one of preferred design. The color of the shutters is another issue. Traditionally, shutters were dark, usually black or dark green. But as time passed, other colors became popular. White and cream became trendy choices for brick and stone houses during the beginning of the twentieth century.

SMART TIP SHUTTER DIPPING

Repainting a shutter with severe paint damage can take much more time and effort than most of us would like. There's no point in doing a little scraping and then adding a new coat of paint. This approach will only last a couple of years. A better approach is to take the shutters to a furniture dipping shop and have the old paint professionally removed.

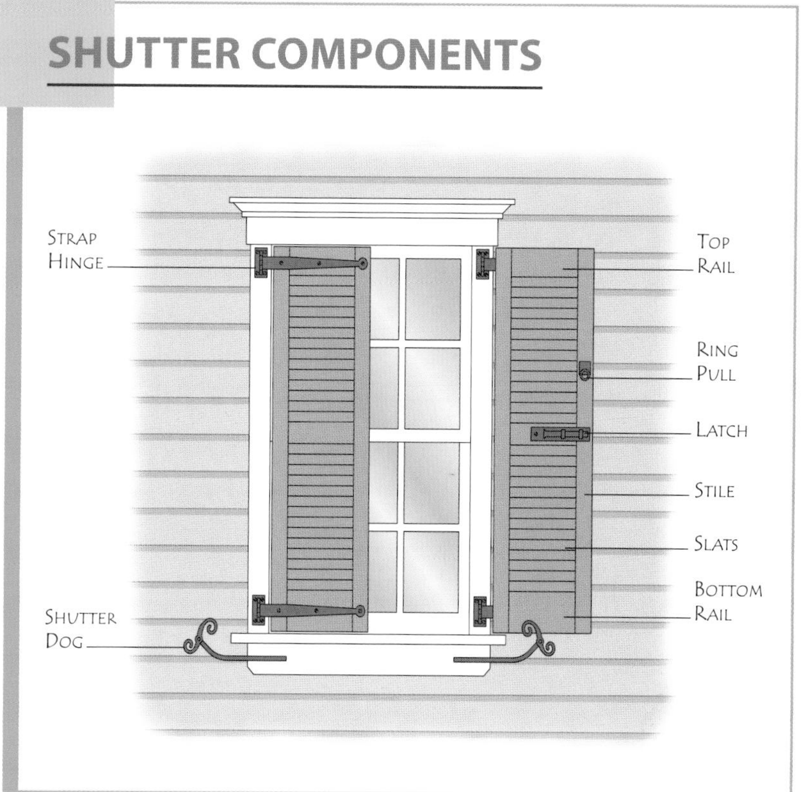
SHUTTER COMPONENTS
Strap Hinge
Top Rail
Ring Pull
Latch
Stile
Slats
Bottom Rail
Shutter Dog

SMART TIP STARTING AT THE TOP

Not all leaks are created equal, especially when it comes to corner boards. A water leak near the bottom of the wall won't do a lot of damage because some of it will drain out at the bottom of the wall. But the same leak at the top of a corner board can result in serious damage, not only to the trim and siding, but also to the wall framing underneath. Damage doesn't take all that much time; a couple of years can make a mess. So check for sound caulking at the tops of the corner boards, and if you ever see damage to the surface of the corner boards, make appropriate repairs right away.

CORNER BOARDS

CORNER BOARDS aren't flashy. Sometimes they have beaded edges, which are nice but not sensational. And often they are painted a contrasting color to the siding boards. Of course, this color is almost always white, again not much of an attention grabber. However, what these plain boards may lack in star power is more than made up for by the crucial weatherproofing role they play.

These trim boards protect the four corners of your house from damage caused by rainwater penetration. They do this by closing the corner (the two boards that form the corner board are caulked and nailed tightly together) and by providing a proper caulking surface for all the siding boards that meet the corner. Because these trim boards are flat, square, and thicker than the siding boards, the cut ends of the siding can tightly abut the corner boards and, when caulked carefully, provide a waterproof joint.

These joints, between the siding and trim boards, are some of the most vulnerable areas to water damage on the walls of any house. The siding itself sheds water effortlessly because each siding board is lapped over the one below. There's no way for water to get inside. But where the siding runs into an obstruction, such as a trim board, the protection by lapping comes to an abrupt halt and caulk becomes the primary protection.

If this caulk fails, some of the water that runs down the side of your house (in a heavy

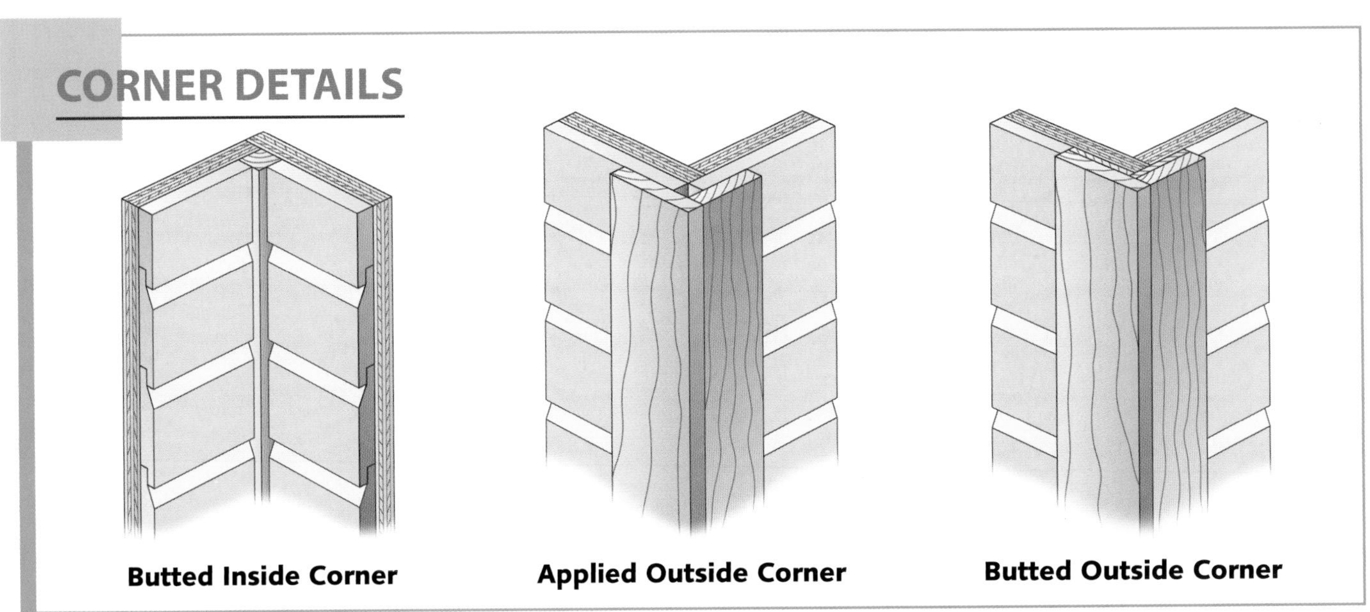

Masonry Corners

MASONRY-SIDED HOUSES, including those covered with brick or stucco, often include decorative quoins at the corners, as shown at right. They can be made of a single large stone or shaped from stucco that is a different color from the rest of the wall. Designers often use quoins of different sizes to create a pattern and provide architectural interest.

rain storm, this can be a lot of water) will easily flow behind the surface. And it will have nowhere to go except be absorbed by the back side of the siding and trim, and the house framing. Once this water is in the wall, the next stop is rot. This process can continue unseen until a great deal of damage has been done.

A DECORATIVE CAP TREATMENT, left, turns this typical corner board into a distinctive design element.

CORNER BOARDS, above, provide a finished look to the edge of a building, and they perform an important waterproofing function as well.

FRIEZES

THE FRIEZE ON THIS HOUSE, above, provides a transition between the brick siding and the overhang of the roof.

IN CLASSICAL ARCHITECTURE, the term frieze refers to one of the trim boards that cover a column-supported beam. These beams are found on porticoes, colonnades, porte cocheres, and practically any front porch on any old house in any town in America. The common usage of the term, however, is much broader than the classical one. When most people refer to a frieze, they mean the wide horizontal board that is installed directly below a soffit. Sometimes this board is just 6 inches wide. But usually it's wider, typically 8 or 10 inches.

A frieze is primarily decorative. Because it falls under an overhang, it doesn't protect any joint that would otherwise be exposed to water damage. The overhang takes care of such things. What a frieze does best is create a solid transition between the siding and the soffit, while at the same time mimicking trim details on the rest of the house. When combined with the corner boards and the water table on an old house, a picture frame of sorts is created for all the siding, giving it a finished, tailored look.

But a frieze isn't just important for a wood-framed and -sided house. Brick and stone houses also use frieze boards for ease-of-construction purposes. Leaving room for

SMART TIP DENTIL CLEANING

Paint failure on a frieze board covered with dentils is almost impossible to scrape clean with a standard paint scraper. One good alternative approach is to use a pressure washer. These machines are inexpensive to rent and are fairly easy to use. But they can be dangerous. The pressure can be so strong at the tip that the stream of water can puncture your skin. You can also damage the trim that's being cleaned. Follow the directions that come with the tool, and when in doubt always err on the side of keeping the tip farther away from the surface.

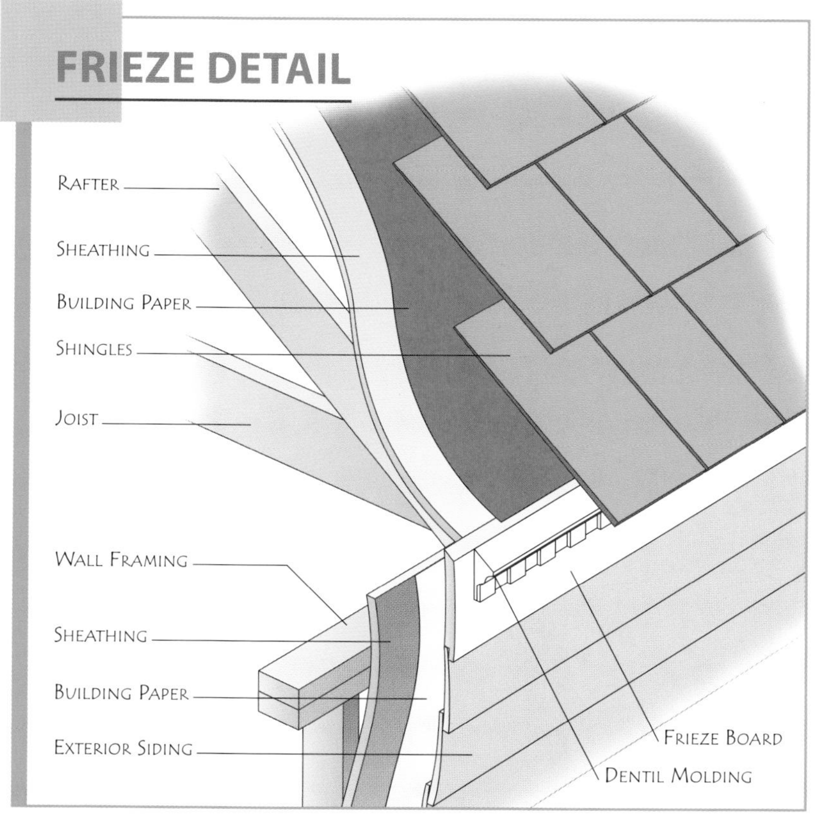

a frieze board between a soffit and the top course of brick or stone makes installing the last foot of masonry much easier.

Occasionally frieze boards have been ornamented with other trim boards, such as a bead along the bottom edge or a cove or crown molding along the top where the frieze meets the soffit. But probably the most common ornaments are dentil moldings. These evenly spaced small blocks have been used in any number of old-house styles where classical detailing was desirable.

THE BUILT-UP FRIEZE, above, adds a nice architectural detail above the group of bay windows on the second floor.

THE FRIEZE around these second-floor windows, **right,** acts as part of the window casing. Note the extra-wide casing near the tops of the middle windows.

Decorative Friezes

ON MOST HOMES, the frieze is usually nothing more than a wide, flat board that serves more as a transition between the siding and the soffit or cornice than a decorative element. But that is not always the case. On Victorian-style homes, designers often use the frieze as a base for distinctive embellishments. Even relatively staid house styles, such as Georgian and Federal designs, sport dentil or egg-and-dart molding over a plain board at the frieze. Here are some possibilities for creating decorative friezes.

CLEVER IDEAS ABOUND for creating decorative friezes. Note how the tree designs, **opposite,** appear to have been cut from the nearby balustrade. A classic design deserves a classic frieze molding treatment, **above left.** Decorative tile was used to create the design on the stucco house shown **left.** When living in a Victorian house, do as the Victorians did, **above;** paint the frieze, and add embellishments.

SMART TIP PEST PATROL

One of the best routes into your house for insects is behind your water table. Because it's close to the ground and usually covered by flowers or bushes, it is usually damp, which is particularly attractive to termites and carpenter ants. Make a routine check for ants and termite tunnels where the water table meets the foundation. If you see any, call an exterminator.

THE CLEVER DESIGN of a water table, **above,** is such that it directs water coming down the wall away from the foundation.

WHEN COMBINED WITH CORNER BOARDS and other trim, **right,** water tables create a frame for the house siding.

WATER TABLES

A WATER TABLE is an exterior trim component that consists of wide horizontal boards installed at the bottom of all the walls. The first course of siding of each wall rests on top of the water table. Typically 8 or 10 inches wide, these boards are used for several reasons. First, they cover the joint between the foundation and the framed house wall, which keeps out air infiltration and discourages insects from taking up a strategic position inside your house. Second, from a design perspective, the strong horizontal statement they make clearly defines the bottom edge of the walls. And third, when topped with a drip cap, these boards direct water that's coming down the side of the house away from the foundation wall below.

Water-Table Features. Water tables are not used only with clapboard siding. They're also frequently installed with veneer

brick and stone siding. One of the clever aspects of a water-table and drip-cap assembly is how the drip cap is designed. It is, of course, wider than the water table so that it can direct the water away from the house. And it has a tapered top edge so the water can't leak back into the joint between the drip cap and the siding. But its most clever feature is the shallow groove that is cut in the underside of the board. This void prevents any water that may migrate across the bottom of the drip cap from reaching the water table. When a drip meets the groove, it falls off.

If the water table and drip cap are working properly, they don't require much maintenance; just keep the paint and caulk in good shape. But keep in mind that these boards are wear items. Because so much water goes over them and because they are splashed by rain hitting the ground next to them, their useful life is shorter than other trim boards.

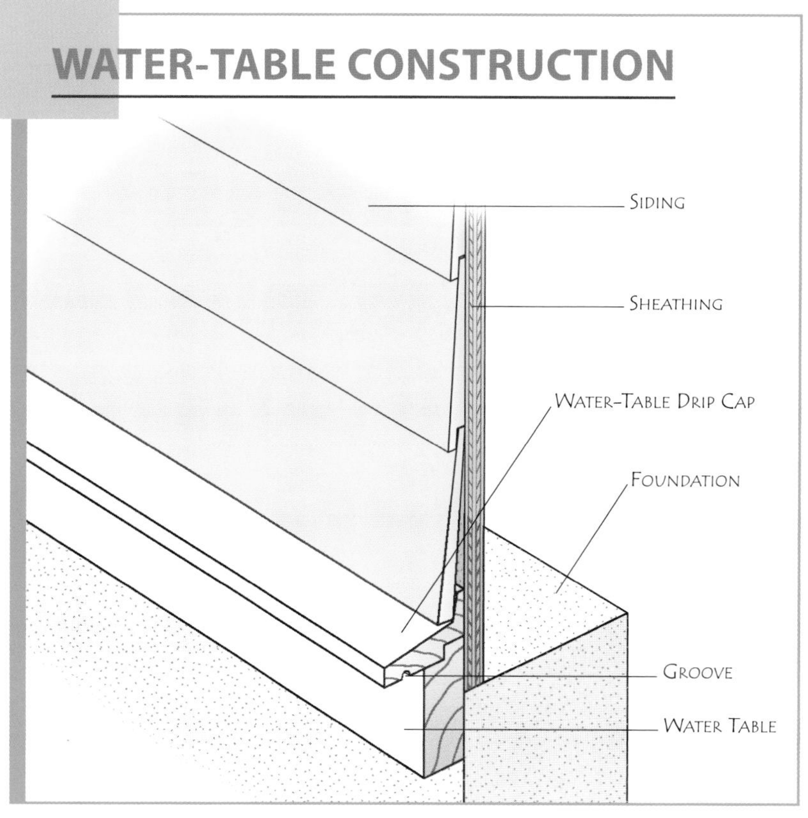

WATER-TABLE TRIM serves as the transition between the foundation and siding, and it makes a strong design statement.

BRACKETS often adorn porches and walls, **above,** of Victorian-inspired house designs.

PILASTERS are ornamental, **below**, but they appear to support part of the structure. Note the pilasters around this window.

PILASTERS, BRACKETS, AND OTHER ELEMENTS

PILASTERS ARE CLASSICAL TRIM DETAILS that fell out of fashion a long time ago. When they were popular, they appeared on any number of different style houses. Georgian, Federal, Greek Revival, and Italianate, to name a few, all made use of these ornaments. Pilasters were designed to look like square pillars that supported the corners of a house. Most were "engaged," which means that they projected just slightly from the facade of the building. In this respect, pilasters look and function like ornate corner boards.

Usually a pilaster is a very wide board with a fluted surface that rests on a base and is topped with a capital. Depending on how substantial they are, pilasters project from the house about 1 to 4 inches. Some of these components are relatively plain, but many grand examples can be found on costly houses. These can feature huge, carved Corinthian capitals that look like inverted bells surrounded by leaves.

Pilasters aren't used only on the corners of a house. Sometimes they are evenly spaced across the front facade to create a bas-relief version of a portico or colonnade. Much more common is the practice of installing smaller pilasters on the sides of the front door, usually next to the sidelights. These are fabricated to the same style as full-size versions. Smaller pilasters are also used to support the back side of small entry porches. In these cases, the pilaster is sometimes structural because it carries some of the load of the porch.

Brackets. Although a staple of Victorian-era porches, brackets made of wood or composite materials can also be found supporting roof overhangs or wedged into the peak of a gable roof on a variety of homes. These elements are usually ornamental but recall a time when exterior support was a necessity in home construction. In most cases today, brackets are simply screwed to the house framing.

Medallions. In the past, only the owners of the grandest house in town could afford a hand-carved wooden medallion or stone inlay on the exterior of their homes. Today, mass production has placed wood and polyurethane medallions and other decorative elements within reach of everyone.

DECORATIVE MEDALLIONS and other embellishments, **below left,** add character to a house design.

ROOF BRACKETS, below right, always appear to be supporting part of the roof. Note the medallion on the porch gable.

CHAPTER 5

PORCHES

A PORCH IS ONE OF THOSE NICE FEATURES almost everybody likes. It also costs a lot of money, which is something that almost no one likes. In fact, porches are so expensive that they were cut out of the plans for most tract homes during the 1960s, '70s and '80s. Leaving porches by the wayside was a good way to make housing a little more affordable and to boost the builder's profits.

These days, porches are making a comeback. Open, screened-in, and glassed-in versions are turning up everywhere, from relatively modest modular homes right up to the stick-built suburban behemoths that are talked about in magazines and on TV. Who doesn't love a porch these days? Apparently, almost no one.

COLUMNS

COLUMNS (AND POSTS) do a lot of work. They hold up most of the porch roof, stabilize the railings, and provide plenty of space for hanging plants, house numbers, hammocks, and more. They are also the first features that register when the porch is seen and thus serve to define the house's architectural style more than most other components. A Greek Revival portico, for example, is going to have tapered, round columns. A Craftsman front porch, on the other hand, would look silly if it didn't have square posts.

Traditionally, columns have been made of wood or stone. Unfortunately, both of these materials are expensive. These days, wood and stone are still popular, but other materials are available too, including fiberglass, aluminum, and polyvinyl chloride (PVC). Many different sizes and shapes are also available. But most fall into two broad categories: round columns and square posts. Each of these categories is further divided into tapered or straight, and fluted or smooth. Many column and post sizes are stock items, but most manufacturers have a custom fabrication service if you need something special.

Caring for Columns. Porch columns may be expensive, but fortunately they are long lasting. Being vertical components, water runs right off them. However, water does stop and splash where it meets the porch floor, which is where most maintenance nightmares occur. Rotted column bases are unavoidable if you have wood columns. Quickly repairing them is important. If the rot goes unchecked for too long, serious structural damage of the column and the floor will result.

COLUMN CONSTRUCTION

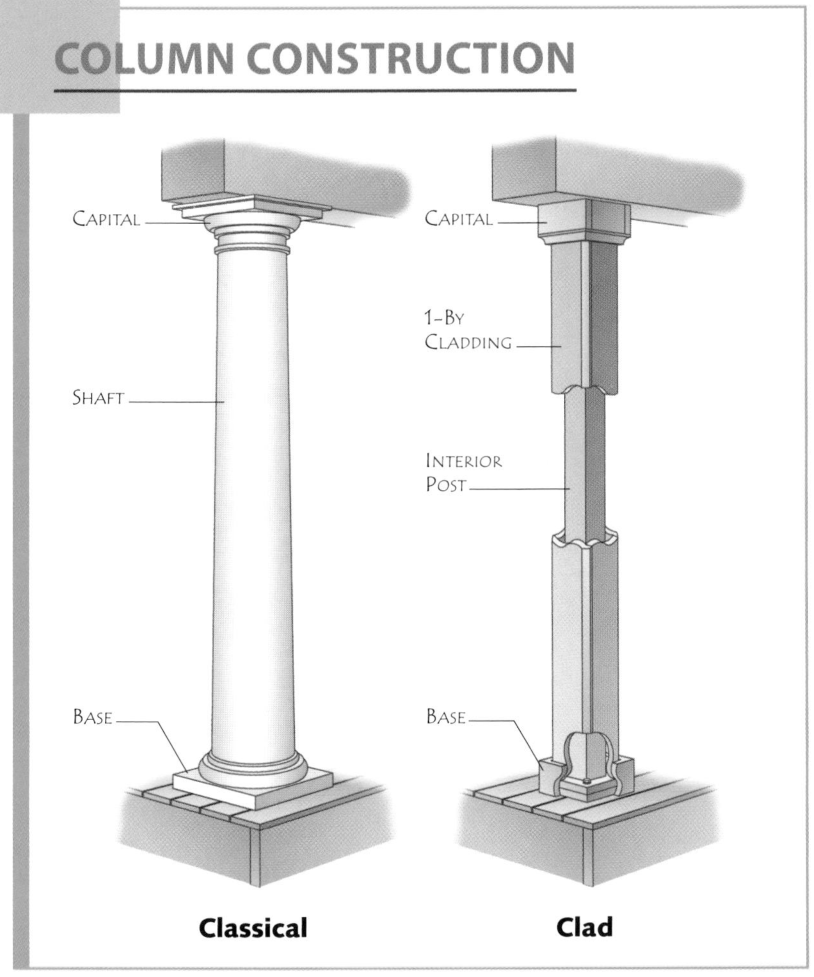

THE DISTINCTIVE DESIGN, opposite, consists of posts connected by lattice and trimwork.

GOOD DESIGN calls for installing an even number of columns across an elevation, **left**.

THE COLUMNS on the porch, **above,** are echoed by smaller versions on the second floor.

Capital Ideas

TO THE ANCIENT GREEKS, columns and the capitals that sat atop them were the perfect expression of the beauty and harmony of the universe. The dimensions of the column's base, the shape and dimensions of the shaft, and the decoration of the capital were governed by strict rules of architecture. Many of these architectural rules are still followed today, although we have become more liberal in columns and capital design. In fact, decorative capitals, or post tops, are a great way to add distinction to a porch.

CLASSIC DORIC-STYLE COLUMNS, opposite left, are topped by simple capitals—a design developed by the ancient Greeks. Brightly painted brackets, **opposite top right,** embellish a post. Carved capitals that break away from the classic styles of columns, **opposite bottom right and top left,** are popular on Victorian-style houses. Corinthian capitals, **top right,** and Ionic capitals, **left,** were developed by the ancient Greeks.

AN UNUSUAL PATTERN adds distinction to these simple balusters. The design complements the simple square porch posts.

PORCH RAILINGS

NOT EVERY PORCH has railings. On old porches the use of railings was a matter of common sense. If the porch was more than a couple of steps high, railings were used to keep everyone from falling off. These days, common sense may still play a role, but when it does it's probably accidental. In new construction, your local ordinances and the building inspector determine the presence or absence of railings, whether it makes sense or not.

Railings (sometimes called balustrades) consist of a top and bottom rail with balusters (spindles) installed between the two. The rails tend to be plain, but the balusters are often more ornate. Turned models are common, and elaborate gingerbread versions appear on Gothic Revival houses and regional vernacular buildings. The more elaborate the railing, the more distinctive the porch. And the more difficult maintenance and repair can be.

Railing Attachment. There are many different ways to attach railings to the columns that support them. The most common is to use some type of hardware screwed to the side of the column and the underside of the rails. The center of longer rails—anything over 6 or 7 feet—is attached to the porch floor with a small block that is screwed to the bottom rail and the floorboards. This block is traditionally painted the same color as the floor so that it blends with the floor.

RAILING STYLES

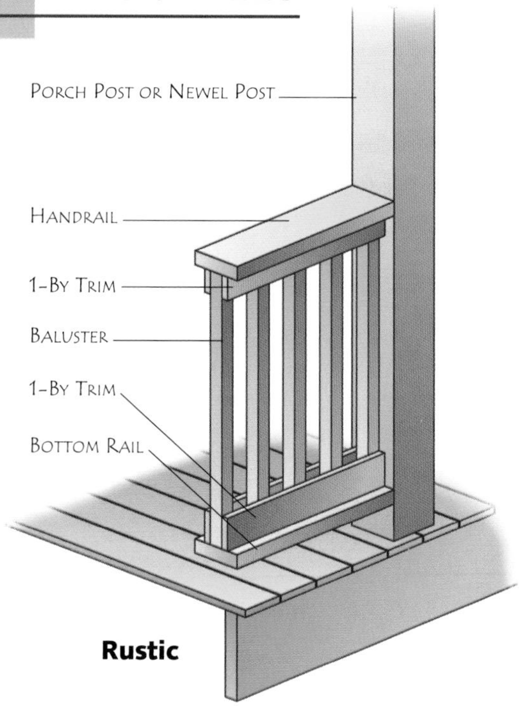

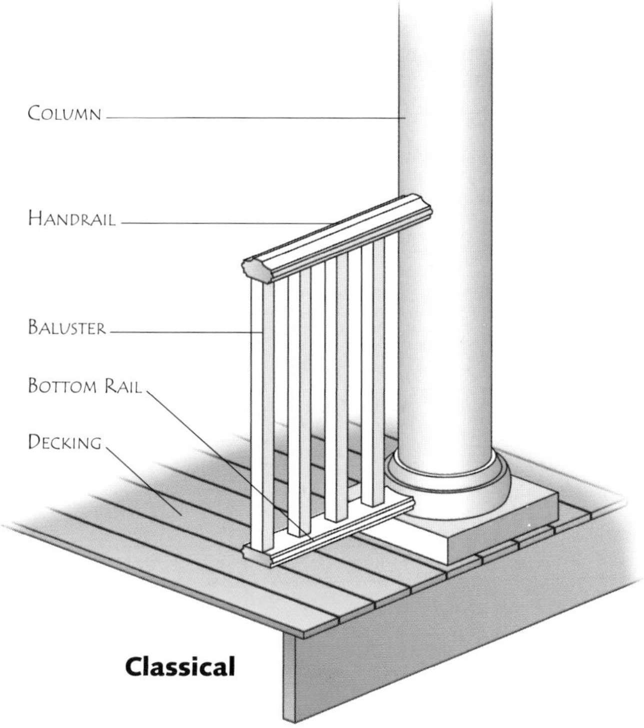

THESE CLASSIC BALUSTERS, above and right, are actually made of polyurethane, eliminating the need for regular maintenance.

WHITE IS THE CLASSIC COLOR, below right, for porch railing systems. In this case, the white balustrade copies the other trimwork on the house.

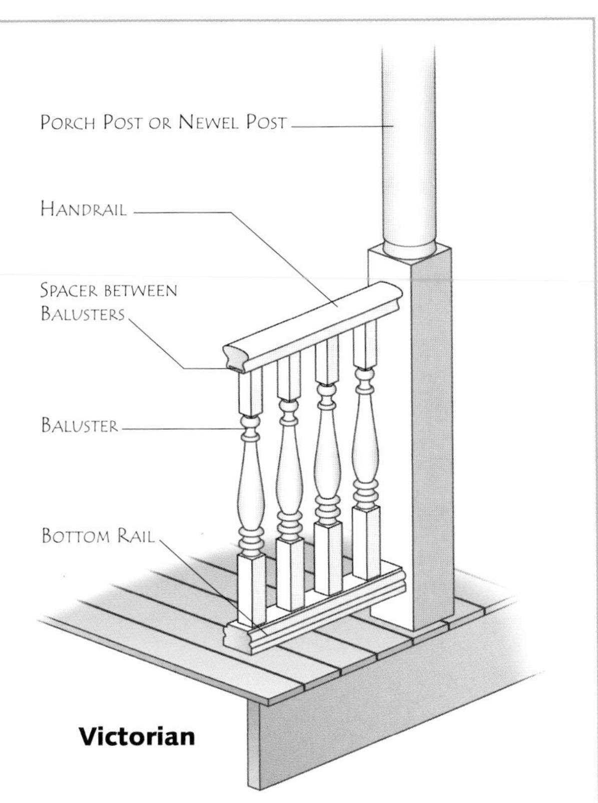

SMART TIP FLUTED COLUMN PREP

Scraping the old paint from fluted porch columns is so difficult that people either give up doing the job or end up damaging the surface from working too vigorously. The best approach to stripping badly cracked and peeling paint is to use paint remover. The remover is just brushed on the column, sits for a time, and then is wiped away. Paint remover, of course, can be used anywhere. But it is expensive when used on large areas.

A BRIGHT COLOR, above, draws attention to this short section of railing.

CHOOSE A RAILING DESIGN, opposite, to complement other trimwork on the house.

THE BALUSTRADE for stairs, **above,** generally continues the design used on the main part of the porch.

BALUSTER DESIGN, right, is not limited to traditional turned wood spindles, as shown here. For a unified look, repeat ornate designs on some other part of the house's trimwork.

Railing Types. Most railings are straight. However, on porches that require railings alongside the steps, these are built to match the angle of the stair stringers. Usually these railings are attached to columns at the top. At the bottom, posts are either anchored in the ground or securely bolted to the side of the stringers to provide rigid support for the railings.

Railing systems are available in a variety of styles and materials. Wood systems are still the standard, but vinyl and polyurethane systems are becoming more and more popular because of the ease of maintenance.

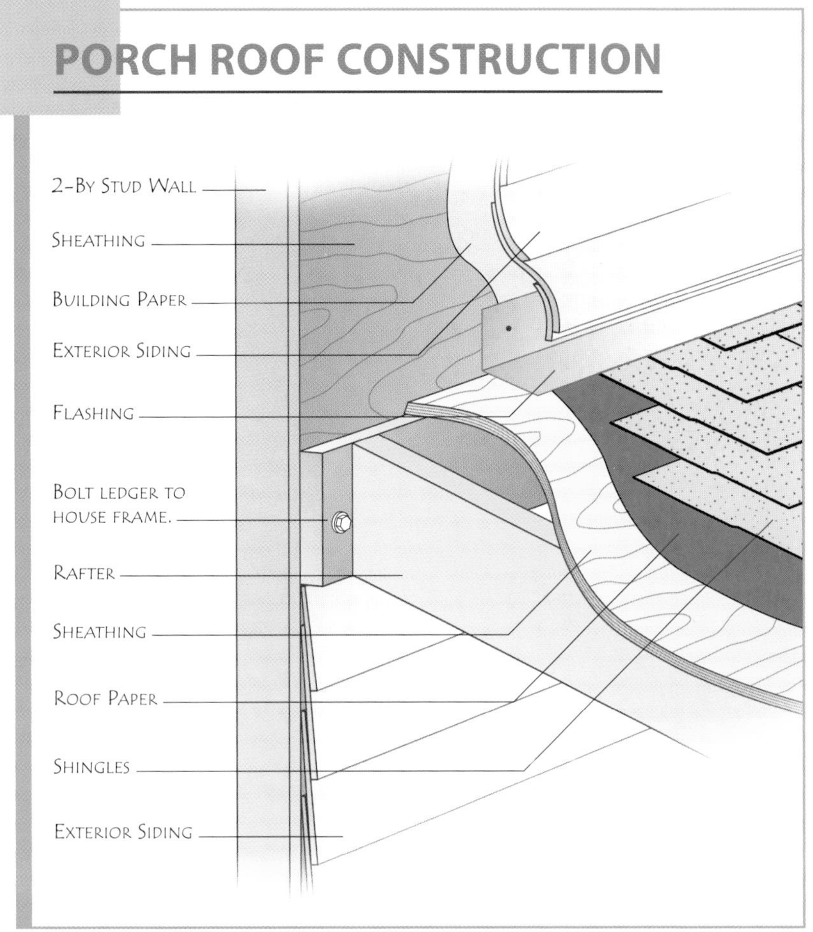

PORCH CEILINGS

Not every porch has a ceiling. Lots of them were built with exposed rafters, beams, wall ties, and roof sheathing boards, but no ceiling joists. If you don't have these joists, there is no place to attach ceiling material. Certainly, there's no structural reason to have a ceiling, but most designs do call for one because they help create a finished appearance.

Ceiling Materials. These days a lot of different materials are used for covering a ceiling, from plain plywood and medium density fiberboard (MDF) to hardboard and PVC panels that simulate beaded boards. But for many older houses, the default material for porch ceilings was beaded wainscoting boards. These tongue-and-groove boards were usually made of fir and were about 3 inches wide. The finished surface was milled to make the single board look like two thinner boards, each with a bead cut along one edge. These

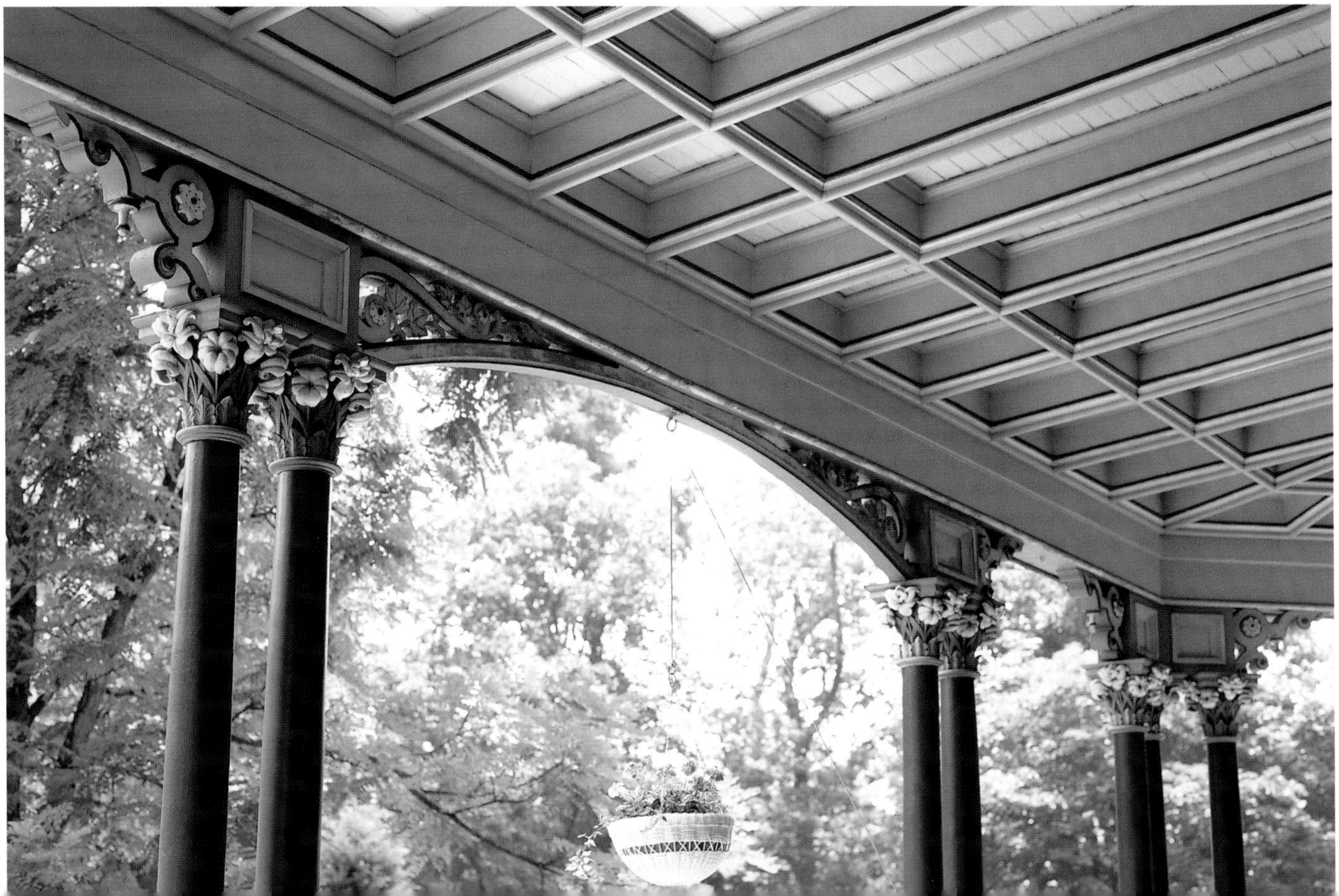

SMART TIP PAINTING BEADED BOARDS

Beaded wainscoting boards look great on a porch ceiling, but they can take a very long time to paint unless you have the right equipment. The right equipment is a 6-foot roller handle and a long-nap roller cover. The handle lets you work from the floor instead of on a ladder. And the deeper nap on the roller cover has longer fibers and holds more paint than a standard roller cover, which makes it easier to reach to the bottom of the grooves formed by the beading.

A CAREFUL PAINT JOB, opposite, created this unusual ceiling treatment. Note how the colors are repeated on the columns.

ALTHOUGH NOT STRUCTURALLY NECESSARY, finished ceilings, **right,** are a nice design touch on traditional porches.

VICTORIAN PORCH CEILINGS, below, are often painted blue to create the feeling of looking at the sky.

boards are still available today, usually on a special-order basis from lumberyards.

Different versions of this material have been used for ages. Some surfaces have V-joints instead of beads. Others have a V-joint on one side and beads on the other. Still other boards are wider (usually no more than 6 inches wide) and have larger beads or V-joints.

The most popular finish for porch ceilings these days is paint, usually white paint. In the past, varnish was more popular than paint. This clear finish aged beautifully and protected the boards sufficiently because they were not exposed to rain and snow. The varnish also allowed the boards to expand and contract with the weather without showing any dark cracks between the boards. White-painted boards, on the other hand, do show these dark cracks until several coats of paint have been applied.

PORCH FLOORS

FLOORS TAKE MORE ABUSE than any other part of a porch. Foot traffic, chair scrapes, and extreme weather exposure all undermine the floor finish. Once the finish is compromised, it doesn't take long for serious damage to start spreading. Exterior horizontal surfaces, such as porch floors, have always been the biggest challenge for any kind of protective coating. Coating manufacturers have responded with their most durable products for this job. For example, alkyd enamels that have high solids content are often called something like "Porch Floor Enamel." When properly applied, these are very good products, but they must be maintained.

In years gone by, 1×4 tongue-and-groove fir boards were one of the most popular materials used for porch floors. These were very straight grained, which made the boards very stable—a real asset in something that was going to be exposed to big swings in temperature and humidity. Unlike the fir boards that were often used for ceilings, fir floorboards were not coated with a clear finish such as varnish. Instead, they were painted.

These days, the traditional fir boards are

TILE IS A FAVORITE, below left, for ground-level designs inspired by the American southwest.

PRESSURE-TREATED LUMBER, below right, has replaced 1x4 tongue-and-groove fir boards for the majority of porch decks.

still available by special order from your local lumberyard. But most builders and contractors use less expensive pressure-treated 1×4 tongue-and-groove boards. Another option is untreated southern yellow pine 1×4 tongue-and-groove boards. Both of these choices are durable and work well for floors, once you get them installed. Unfortunately, both have unruly grains that lead to twists and warps. Installing them so that they look good takes a lot of time and effort.

Some of the new generation of recycled and composite decking boards can also be used on porches, although some materials have specific installation requirements that are different from wood. However, these materials are not used on porches as often as alternative materials are used for railing systems.

No matter what material is used, each board should be primed on all six sides before it's installed. (If the back priming is omitted, short-term paint failure is almost a certainty.) And once the installation is complete, the whole floor should be coated with one or two topcoats of paint, depending on the manufacturer's recommendations printed on the can.

A PAINTED FINISH, below, is the best treatment for wood porch flooring. Be sure to use paints formulated for porches.

Decorative Trimwork

PORCHES ARE GREAT PLACES to add decorative elements that might look out of place on other parts of the house. These elements include distinctive railing systems, brackets, gingerbread detailing, and the like. In most cases, these elements have no structural purpose, and they are usually installed by simply screwing the element to the porch structure. They can be made of wood or one of the newer generation of plastics.

ORNAMENTAL EMBELLISHMENTS can unify a design as is the case with the trimwork accents installed between the posts on the porches shown here, **all this page**. Note how the design in the medallion shown **above** is repeated on the stair risers. A sunburst design completes an arched detail, **opposite top left.** Small spindles accent a porch design, **opposite top right.** A wagon-wheel design creates a design theme, **opposite bottom left.** Note the cutouts, **opposite bottom right.**

PIER SCREENS

ALTHOUGH HIDDEN BY THE SHRUBS, below, this porch sits atop a foundation wall. It is best to install vents in foundation sidewalls.

LATTICE PIER SCREENS, opposite left, have a finished appearance, and they allow the flow of air to the area under the porch

ORNATE PORCHES, opposite right, often have ornate pier screens to complement the design. Note the custom detailing of the screen.

MOST PORCHES are built on piers or posts and are elevated off the ground by a few feet. The height of an individual porch is established by the height of the floor inside the house. Generally speaking, the porch floor is built either to match the floor height inside or to be one step lower (about 7 to 8 inches) than the house floor. The relationship between the two floors is based on safety. If they are the same height, people won't trip. If they are one step different, people will be unlikely to trip because 8-inch-high steps are common everywhere. But if the change in height is 4 inches, for example, stumbles are sure to follow.

A raised porch doesn't present any real problems; you have to go up stairs to reach the front door whether there's a porch in place or not. But it does create a visible gap between the piers, which is usually covered by some sort of wood screen. Often made of lattice, these screens are designed to give the porch a finished look and also to keep large animals from setting up house under the floor.

Long-Lasting Materials. The biggest drawback to using these wood screens is that they rot quickly, a result of their location. Being so close to the ground, and often covered with plantings, makes for a damp environment. Fortunately, today there are better material options for these screens, and you don't have to look far. Home centers carry PVC lattice, with diagonal or square patterns, in several different colors, as well as pressure-treated lattice panels.

On some porches there's no need for lattice at all because the floor sits on top of a continuous foundation wall. This is a high-quality way to build a porch, especially if you may want to close it in some day and use it for year-round living space.

SMART TIP BUILDING PIER SCREENS

Making a replacement screen for your porch isn't very difficult. The easiest approach is to use pressure-treated lattice and pressure-treated 1x4s. Cut and join the 1x4s into a simple frame. Then cut the lattice panel about 1 inch shorter and 1 inch narrower than the frame. Nail or screw the lattice onto the back of the frame, and prime and paint the assembly. When everything is dry, nail the screen to the rim joist of the porch floor and to the foundation posts. To create access to the under-porch area, install strap hinges along the top of the frame.

Pier Screen Construction

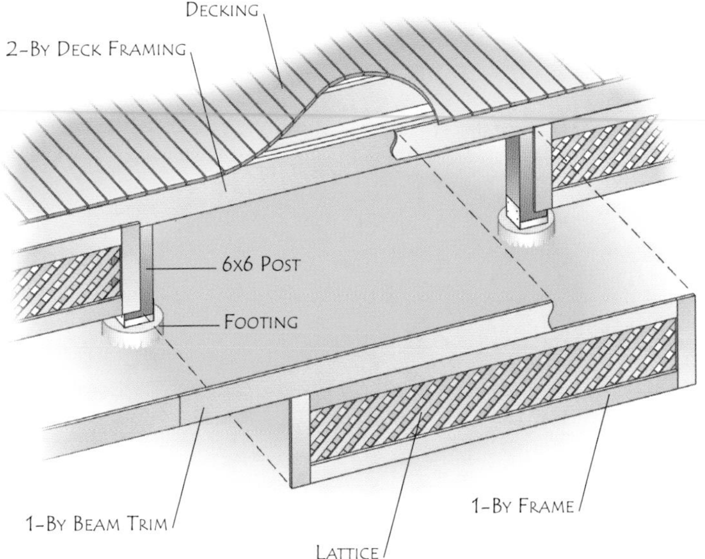

PORCH STEPS

PORCH STEPS aren't only a good way to move up in the world. They're also a great place to sit and watch the world go by, talk to the neighbors, and have a cup of coffee or maybe a drink after work. Of course, the bigger the steps are, the more people that can fit on them, and the more people there are, the more fun there is to be had.

On older houses, the front steps were almost always given special treatment. They were wider than necessary, and they often had shorter risers so they were easier to climb. Also, the handrails on both sides were

SMART TIP LEVELING STEPS

If the steps on your porch are leaning to one side or the other, you should shim them until they are level. First, check the steps by holding a level across the bottom tread and noting how high one end of the level has to be raised for the bubble to reach the middle. This is the thickness of the shim that is needed. Then cut up several pieces of asphalt roofing shingles (about 12 inches square each) until the stack you have matches the thickness you need. Use a flat bar or a wrecking bar to pry up the low corner. Then slide the pile underneath so the stringer sits on the shingles. Check the tread with the level again, and add more shingles if necessary.

usually the same kind of decorative balustrades that were used for the porch railings. On masonry porches, the steps could be truly ornate with large carved banisters on both sides and curving balustrades that ended in stone porch columns.

Wood Steps. On wood porches, the steps are built independently of the porch floor and are usually installed as an assembly. The sidepieces are called stringers, the vertical boards between the steps are called risers, and the boards you actually step on are called treads. Once these components are joined together, the assembly is nailed to the front of the porch floor.

Many of the long-term problems that steps suffer are the result of how they are supported. The top of the steps is nailed to the porch, which is usually supported by piers or posts that go down below the frost line. If the ground heaves during cold weather, the porch and the top of the steps don't move. But the bottom of the steps is often just sitting on the ground or a section of sidewalk. Both of these can and do move up and down during cold weather. Over time, this stress damages the steps. Poor support can also harm steps in warm climates, where the ground under the steps settles but the support under the porch does not.

STONE STEPS set into the hillside, **opposite left,** lead to this unique circular porch or covered patio.

STAIR POSTS AND BALUSTRADES, opposite right, offer the opportunity to express yourself.

WRAPAROUND STAIRS, below, add design interest and extra seating space to this porch.

ENCLOSED PORCHES

THE DEFAULT AMERICAN PORCH is unquestionably open to the air. That's the point. One goes out to the porch like one goes to a destination resort, to feel the cool air, a breeze here and there, and to let time and care slip away. Sometimes you can even get a dry, front-row seat to a virtuoso lightening storm. All of this is available without getting in the car and leaving home. Now that's hard to beat.

It may be hard to beat most of the time, but not all of the time—not when it's cold, or snowing, or drenched with driving rain. For these conditions and others, enclosed porches were created. They come in two basic types: screened-in and glassed-in. The screened examples are top performers when it comes to battling bugs and rain. But for ultimate versatility, the choice has to be the glass model. With many big windows, these

SMART TIP HEATING THINGS UP

Figuring out if your current furnace has the capacity to heat another room is complicated and best left to a professional at your local utility or fuel supplier. If the answer is no, there are still plenty of auxiliary heat options you can investigate. Wood and pellet stoves are still popular but not the most convenient options. More convenient are the gas and oil appliances that boast a very wide range of BTU outputs. They are also available in ventless, direct-vent, and flue-vent models. Discuss with your heater retailer which vent is best for the room you want to heat.

porches have almost as much light as an open structure. And when all the windows are open and screens are installed, the room can catch errant breezes that come along, while keeping bugs out.

Enclosure Types. At first glance, these porches look very similar, the only real difference being screen walls versus glass walls. But one is simple (the screened option) and the other is complicated (the glassed version). A screened-in porch is nothing more than an open porch with some screened panels nailed in place around its perimeter. But a glassed-in porch needs perimeter walls with insulation and heavy windows nailed in place. And it needs lots of insulation in the ceiling and the floor if it's going to be used during the cold months. Plus, it needs a source of heat, either a warm-air duct from the house or auxiliary heat from something like a gas fireplace or stove. Adding the heat isn't hard, but adding the insulation is difficult and expensive.

MANY ENCLOSED PORCHES, opposite top, contain both windows and screens for year-round enjoyment.

SCREENED PORCHES, opposite bottom, have a homey feel to them. Many serve as back or side porches.

ENCLOSED PORCHES, above, provide the opportunity to enjoy the scenery without being exposed to the elements.

CREATING AN ENCLOSED PORCH, right, is a relatively inexpensive way to add usable living area to your home.

FLOOR FRAMING

STRICTLY SPEAKING, floor framing is not a part of exterior trim. It may be what a lot of trim is nailed to, but it isn't trim. It isn't exactly regular framing, either. In your house, all the framing falls within the exterior envelope of the building. It's always covered by things such as sheathing, siding, and roofing. Because of this, builders and contractors can use relatively inexpensive spruce, pine, or fir for framing and not worry about exposure to the weather. In fact, if traditional framing is exposed to moisture, it can start to rot.

This exposure can be from either direct contact with water or prolonged contact with water vapor. If the wood doesn't have a chance to dry out between doses, then rot sets in. If it can dry out, then there's no problem; this is how traditional porch floor framing works. Because the beams, joists, and flooring are exposed to open air, albeit near the ground, they can stay dry. So there was no need to use rot-resistant lumber or, in the old days, to coat the framing with a preservative such as creosote.

Rot-Resistant Framing. This method of construction assumes that the porch floor will always function as a waterproof barrier on the top of the structure. Of course, this isn't always true. Failure in the floor coating and boards causes many a joist to rot. Fortunately, there's a good solution to this problem, namely pressure-treated framing lumber. This material is more expensive than common lumber, and it's certainly harder to work with. But used in a porch floor, it should last indefinitely.

Pressure-treated lumber, as well as the fasteners needed for installation, are a stock item in lumberyards and home centers. Any time a structural repair is required on a porch, use this lumber. It's like buying a little insurance policy against future damage.

ALTHOUGH PORCH FRAMING IS COVERED, below right, it can get wet and needs a means to dry out, such as the lattice pier screens shown here.

MOST PORCH FRAMING, opposite, is constructed using pressure-treated lumber for long-lasting protection.

SMART TIP PROTECT YOURSELF

Exposure to pressure-treated lumber is far from lethal. But the preservative in it is also far from benign. The best approach is to protect yourself and others when you use it. The first line of defense is protective clothing and accessories. Wear long pants and a long-sleeved shirt, gloves, safety glasses, and a dust mask when cutting, sanding, and drilling the material. Never let children play around the site when this material is being used. After the project is done, thoroughly rake up or sweep up all the sawdust and dispose of it, along with any scraps of the wood. Check with your local health department to find out where to take this waste.

CHAPTER 6

TRIMWORK FOR OUTBUILDINGS

THESE DAYS MOST PRODUCTION HOUSES look a little lonely on their ¼-acre building lots. They don't have remote garages, to say nothing of barns or other outbuildings; some of the storage sheds that pop up here and there look like afterthoughts; and the outhouses that moved inside a long time ago are barely remembered. But many old houses don't suffer this isolation. The family house represents just the official center of the operation, but not all the living stays within those walls. Ask the kids who have a separate garage, shed, or barn where they spend their free time. For these kids, and maybe their parents too, outbuildings can be a lot of fun. After all, not many people bounce a basketball in the living room, but how many can resist doing it in the garage?

GARAGES

DETACHED GARAGES may be a thing of the past in new construction, but there are plenty of old ones around. And not everyone who has to walk through the rain to get to the car is unhappy about it. There are a couple of good reasons for this. First, most detached garages are bigger than their attached counterparts. Of course there are lots of little, one-car boxes behind 60s production houses. But these are more than offset by all the small barns that populate the backyards of houses built between the 1860s and the 1960s. And second, remote garages let people store explosive and combustible items farther away than the other side of the kitchen door. Keeping things like gasoline, kerosene, paint thinner, and paint remover inside the house (which is what an attached garage is) is a bad idea.

Trim Designs. Many old garages take their design cues from the house. This can yield wonderful results, like when a Gothic Revival garage, complete with ornate bargeboards, adorns the backyard of a large Gothic Revival house. These buildings can look more like guest cottages than simple garages. And the duplication of trim treatments should be maintained whenever the garage is remodeled.

On detached garages that don't share the house design, the differences should be played down. For example, if the house is painted a dark color but has white trim, consider using the same paint scheme on the garage. The trim treatment may not match, but the paint scheme will blunt the difference. Another option is to simply paint the entire garage a neutral color. This will tend to make all the features in the garage blend together. This will also minimize the difference between the house and garage, especially if the color for the garage appears somewhere on the house.

SMART TIP DOOR OPENERS

Many older garages have overhead doors but don't have garage door openers. Installing openers is a straightforward, do-it-yourself job that should take less than a weekend. The first requirement is that the garage needs to have electricity. If you have lights in the garage, you're in business. The second requirement is an opener. A good choice for most jobs is a ½-hp model. These are available at hardware stores and home centers and come with complete installation instructions.

DECORATIVE HARDWARE, opposite top, can add a distinctive look to garage doors.

THIS THREE-CAR GARAGE, opposite bottom, has the detailing of a modern barn.

THE BARGE BOARD on the garage **above** could easily be used on the main house.

SMART TIP SHED PLANS

If you're interested in building a storage shed, there's plenty of help out there. There are many books available on the subject, including Creative Homeowner's *Ultimate Guide to Yard & Garden Sheds,* which takes you through the process of building five sheds and offers shed plans for sale. Remember to check with your local building department before starting work. Many towns, even in rural areas, require a building permit for a storage shed.

STORAGE SHEDS

MOST STORAGE SHEDS are more about price and convenience than about design. The idea is to put up something quickly that will hide things like the lawn mower, and all the extra dog food that was on sale last month. Many sheds are the product of deep-thinking marketing people who can often come up with something that's cheap, but not so often something that's attractive. There's not much that can be done about this, short of painting the shed a tasteful color.

Another option is to buy a locally (or regionally) made storage shed. These small buildings are available in about as many dif-

THIS SHED, with its eye-catching saltbox roofline, was custom designed for this property. It has simple 1x4 window and door casings and roof trim.

ferent designs as there are people building them. Usually, the shed is completed and then moved to the buyers lot on a truck with a tilting bed. Minor site preparations are required. But once the shed is in place, it's ready to use. Hiring a contractor to build a shed that complements your house is the most expensive option. But it does give you the chance to specify exactly the trim, siding, and roofing details you want.

But, not everyone has to buy a new storage shed. Older houses often have small garden sheds on the property, just simple structures to keep gardening tools close at hand. The best of these buildings duplicate the trim style on the house. Generally the rakes, corner boards, fascias, etc., are scaled down to a size that looks appropriate.

Though these buildings can be beautiful, many of them have one big problem. They were placed directly on the ground, or close to it, and this caused rot in the floor beams and the lower siding boards. Even when these were placed on large corner stones, rain splashing and piles of snow kept the wood members wet for long periods. Because of this, when a shed has rotting problems, it makes sense to raise the whole structure at least one foot above the ground and to replace the floor framing and water-table trim with pressure-treated lumber.

SHEDS ARE USUALLY HARD WORKING, but they can add a touch of style to your yard. The simple garden shed, **top,** features an unusual gable window. The trimwork of the shed shown **center** allows it to be placed within view of the street. The nautical motif of the shed at **right** suits its role as storage for pool supplies.

Decorative Outbuildings

NOT ALL SMALL OUTBUILDINGS are used for storage. Some function as playhouses for the kids, guest houses, retreats to get away from it all, or just an element to decorate the yard. Many are custom designed to either mimic the main house—complete with porches, chimneys, and working windows—or to complement the look in some way. Others can be purchased through shed manufacturers.

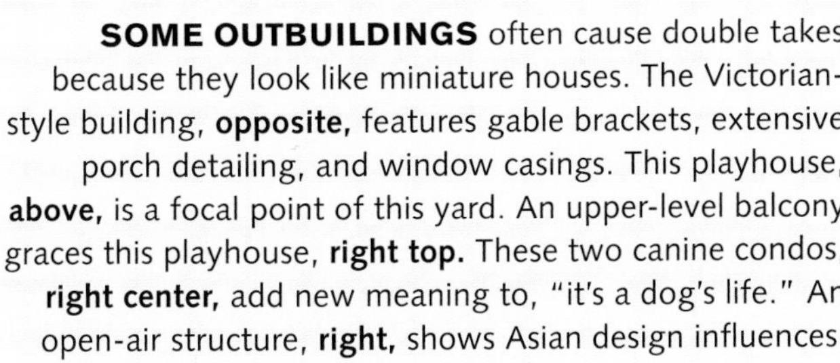

SOME OUTBUILDINGS often cause double takes because they look like miniature houses. The Victorian-style building, **opposite,** features gable brackets, extensive porch detailing, and window casings. This playhouse, **above,** is a focal point of this yard. An upper-level balcony graces this playhouse, **right top.** These two canine condos, **right center,** add new meaning to, "it's a dog's life." An open-air structure, **right,** shows Asian design influences.

BARNS

A BARN IS PRETTY HARD TO DEFINE. Most of us would agree that it's bigger than a storage shed and smaller than an airline terminal. But it's those buildings in between that cause the confusion. In rural areas, the gambrel behemoths that anchor the surrounding farmland would seem to fit the bill, without question. But what of the two-story building, not ten miles away, that's sitting behind an old house in the middle of town. The people who own it call it a barn and who wants to argue with them?

Construction Basics. No matter what the definition, barns are almost always built to lower standards than the houses they accompany. Barns typically have poorer foundations, cruder siding, and almost nonexistent trim. But this isn't true of all barns. A good rule of thumb is: the bigger the barn the coarser the construction. The smaller barns, particularly those located in town, were often built to look much like the house. These buildings are real gems and add significantly to the value of any property.

Because of their size, barns can be hard to maintain. It's easier to postpone a paint job when it's going to be so expensive. And, inevitably, a one-year delay turns into several years. Similarly, it's easy to stall a re-roofing job. But without a solid water barrier on the roof, the structure is being condemned to a shorter life. Barn maintenance is a good destination for some of the home equity that's piling up on your financial statement.

Don't forget: one person's backyard barn is another person's guesthouse or rental property. So, the building you maintain today may pay off at sale time more than the brick walkway you installed in front or the privacy fence you built out back.

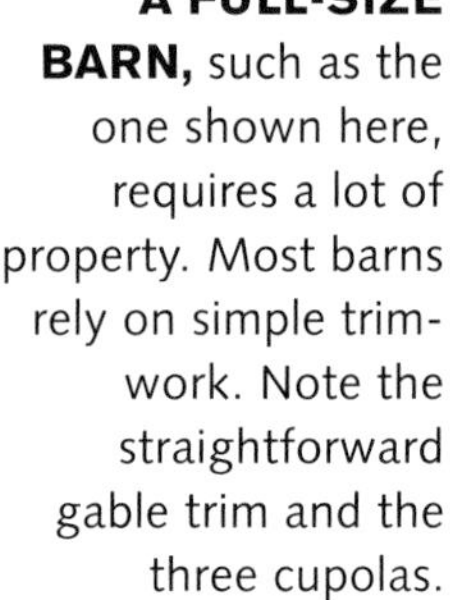

A FULL-SIZE BARN, such as the one shown here, requires a lot of property. Most barns rely on simple trimwork. Note the straightforward gable trim and the three cupolas.

SMART TIP SPRAY PAINTING

Any large building can eat up a lot of paint, especially if the surface is rough, which can often be the case with heavily weathered barns. One way to cut these costs is by spray painting with an airless sprayer. This tool is a common rental item and not very expensive to buy (about $100). Because it doesn't use a compressor, the tool is easy to use and has very little overspray. It puts on a more uniform layer of paint than brushing or rolling methods and takes much less time.

YARD AND GARDEN SHEDS that look like barns, **right,** are a common sight in suburban yards.

A RUSTIC BARN, below, commands center stage and provides necessary storage in this large garden.

GAZEBOES

GAZEBOES HAVE HAD A LONG, ILLUSTRIOUS LIFE in American residential design. First appearing in large numbers with the Victorian styles of the mid-nineteenth century, this structure endures today in the backyards of simple homes and eye-popping mansions alike. Its distinctive shape (usually hexagonal or octagonal) identifies it immediately as something special, like an architectural folly in the English countryside.

A SCREENED-IN GAZEBO, with an ornate double roof that contains additional venting, is a welcome destination in any yard. Note the multiple doors.

In many cases, particularly the gazeboes that were built when the house was built, these structures were designed to be extensions of the porch. They were also built as separate rooms attached to other parts of the house with a covered walkway. Because they were built at the same time, the construction details on the gazebo matched those of the house. The same size fascias, posts, railings, etc. were used on the gazebo, but they were often embellished more. Plain overhangs sprout sturdy brackets, columns have bases and capitols with carved details, and railings have turned spindles that don't appear on the porch rails.

Building a gazebo as part of a porch is difficult because it's such an atypical shape. Certainly, sophisticated carpentry skills are required. But adding a gazebo to an existing porch is even harder because good carpentry skills must be wed to good architectural skills to make everything look okay. As a result, most gazeboes these days are built away from the house, like small pavilions.

These structures are often screened in and located in shady sections of the yard. Many are site built; many others are built from kits. And some are built off-site and delivered by a truck with a tilting bed that just drops the gazebo in place. Big national outfits compete with small local or regional builders. Local builders might charge more, but you should be able to specify construction and trim details that would match those on your house.

IN ADDITION TO PROVIDING A SHADY RETREAT, opposite top, the trimwork on this gazebo makes it a garden focal point.

ROOF TRIM, A DECORATIVE BALUSTRADE, AND PIER SCREEN, opposite bottom, give this gazebo the look of an ornate porch.

GREENHOUSES

FOR GARDENING ENTHUSIASTS, it's hard to beat a greenhouse. It provides all-year, all-weather gardening no matter where you live, almost. (Arctic areas may have to settle for frozen food and flowers.) Greenhouses also provide a great retreat, a quiet place to focus on plants, not animals. But gardening isn't the only reason to have a greenhouse. Many of these buildings serve as family rooms, home offices, and home gyms. And not all greenhouses are separate structures. Many are attached to the house in the form of sunrooms, while others are modest bump outs, like big bay windows, that provide room for eating space in the kitchen.

Construction Differences. Because many of these structures have metal frames (usually aluminum) they don't often have trim details that are used on a house. There are no rake boards, bargeboards, soffits, friezes, nor water tables. These structures don't need the weatherproofing function of trim, and adding the design aspects of trim would cost too much. If the greenhouse is close to the house, the difference in design looks awkward. When the greenhouse is farther away, closer to the garden for exam-

SMART TIP HEATING GREENHOUSES

If you live in a cool climate, greenhouses and conservatories are good for any number of reasons. But they do have one shortcoming: they need heat. When the sun is out and the weather is warm, there's heat to spare. But when it's cold, no matter how long the sun shines each day, there's not enough heat to keep the room usable for people or plants. You have to add some. But reference to this heat (or more precisely, the cost of this heat) is rarely discussed during a sales pitch. So it's your responsibility to nail down heating estimates for your locale, and to include these in the cost of a greenhouse or conservatory before you make your purchase decision.

STAND-ALONE GREENHOUSES, left top, make excellent potting sheds, but they can trap an enormous amount of heat. These structures are attractive but require additional ventilation.

ADD-ON GREENHOUSES OR SUNSPACES, left center, are not really outbuildings, but they are a great way to add living space. Most sunspaces are semi-custom kits installed by the manufacturer.

ple, the lack of house design elements is hardly noticed.

One alternative to a typical greenhouse is the upscale conservatories that are becoming standard equipment on expensive houses. These beautiful structures have all the architectural trim detailing that greenhouses lack. They also have astonishing price tags; many cost more than $50,000. Conservatories became popular in eighteenth-century Europe, particularly in England. In those days, they were used as greenhouses for growing food and were sometimes called orangeries, or places to grow orange trees. These days, using such an expensive room for producing a few tomatoes and tulips seems almost quaint. Conservatories are almost always used as sunrooms or libraries.

WHILE NOT TECHNICALLY A GREENHOUSE, this shed dormer, with its wall of glass, accomplishes the same goals, with great views as a bonus.

ARBORS

ARBORS COME IN DIFFERENT SHAPES AND STYLES and are installed in different locations. Their primary task is to support crawling vines, so they are generally constructed of lattice within a sturdy framework. Arbors are frequently positioned at the entrance to a garden, and sometimes located as a destination point in the garden if the arbor has a bench or swing inside.

Other common spots are near the back or side doors, where the arbor functions as a modest pergola. Both structures have similar purposes—to support vegetation. But the arbor is smaller and more intimate, and it takes less time for plant material to cover it. Arbors are not usually considered part of the house trim, unless, for example, they serve as a kind of lattice colonnade between the back door and the garage. These larger structures can have railings along the sides that match the house. And the occasional roof can share house roof trim details.

Privacy Screens. These are very similar to arbors in construction if not in purpose. Both have sturdy frames that support lattice panels. And both are secured at the bottom to keep them from falling over. These screens are sometimes elements of porch construction, usually placed at an end that is too close to the neighbors. Other times their job is more prosaic: they cover the garbage cans or hide unsightly spots like compost beds.

If you are building (or having built) an arbor or privacy screen, it's a great opportunity to incorporate trim details from the house into the design. For example, if your front porch has tapered columns, then use smaller versions of these columns to support the arbor or screen. And, if your window trim features head casings with cove molding along the top, then use cove molding along the top edge (or all around) the lattice frame.

A PRIVACY SCREEN forms a pleasant backdrop for a garden bench. Note the repeating corner design on the screens.

A FLOWER-COVERED ARBOR, opposite left, frames the entrance to this private garden retreat. Arbors often serve as transition structures.

GARDEN SCREENS, opposite top right, can provide privacy when covered with vines or flowers and often serve as boundary markers.

GARDEN ARBORS, opposite bottom right, often contain benches or other seating and provide a shady retreat in the yard.

SMART TIP CHOOSING VINES

If you have an arbor but don't have a vine on it, you have a little research to do. Not every plant works in every location. Your best source for where plants will live and flourish is the USDA Hardiness Zone tables. The plant grower specifies the acceptable zone in the form of a number and then you match the number to a map of the country (www.usna.usda.gov) that shows where each zone is located. If you are in that zone, then the plant should work. You'll also have to check the light requirements the plant needs. Some like full sun, others like full shade, and others like everything in between.

CHAPTER 7

HOUSE SIDING

IF YOU'RE GOING TO CONSIDER EXTERIOR HOUSE TRIM, it's impossible to omit a discussion of the most prominent varieties of siding because the two features are fundamentally related. Not only are their appearances related, but also the proper installation of each element is dependent on the way their intersection is treated. Each wall opening, such as a window or door, as well as inside and outside corners, soffits, and rakes, presents a potential spot for water to cross the protective barrier that siding and trim are meant to represent. So, while the trim and siding must work together on an aesthetic level, it is also important that these intersections are engineered to allow the individual elements to expand and contract as necessary and still offer the requisite protection from wind, rain, and snow.

WOOD CLAPBOARD

CLAPBOARD is one of the most popular horizontal styles of siding, falling into the broader category known as "beveled" or "lap" siding. The individual boards are cut in a tapered profile and installed so that each row overlaps the next lower course by 1 to 2 inches. The most common wood varieties that are used for clapboard siding are cedar and redwood, providing the choice of finishing with paint, solid or semitransparent stain, or clear water-repellent sealers. Less expensive alternative materials are pine or spruce, but these species are not suitable for clear or semitransparent finishes.

Clapboard Types. Clapboards are sold in various widths from 4 to 12 inches, providing a range of design options with the same material. The best quality material is cut from clear lumber and exhibits a quarter-sawn grain pattern, called "clear, vertical grain." While this grade of siding is more expensive than flat-grain stock, it expands and contracts much less with seasonal changes in temperature and humidity and therefore will hold a finish longer. For a paint-grade job, it's often possible to order clapboard stock that is factory-primed, eliminating the need for the installer to back-prime the siding—except for field cuts.

For a first-quality installation, wood clapboard should be installed with nails that resist corrosion; stainless-steel siding nails are considered the best choice. Nails should be driven so that the heads are just flush to the wood surface, not countersunk, for best holding power and least chance of splitting the siding stock. Inside and outside corners are often finished with corner boards, although metal outside corner caps can be used for a painted finish. Tight miter joints

NAILING CLAPBOARD

Stud Wall
Building Paper
Sheathing
Clapboard
Subfloor
Joist
Joist Header
Starter Strip
Sill Plate
Sill Seal
Foundation

on outside corners are difficult to achieve and rarely hold up to the stress of weather exposure.

Wood clapboard is widely considered to be a first-class siding material. When properly installed and maintained, it can last indefinitely, often with improved appearance as it ages. Of course, these features come at a substantial cost, as both the material and installation costs are relatively high when compared with other products. And you need to be prepared to maintain and renew the finish on the siding as it weathers.

WOOD SIDING WORKS BEST when installed on a traditional-style house, such as the one shown **below,** or an Arts and Crafts-inspired design.

SOLID WOOD CLAPBOARD, opposite top, provides an attractive finish to exterior walls. When properly maintained, clapboard siding will last for years.

PAINTED FINISHES abound for wood clapboard. The houses shown **opposite bottom** were painted in a Victorian-style color scheme. Choose the colors that best suit the style of the house.

SHINGLES & SHAKES

WOOD SHINGLES AND SHAKES are popular for the rustic style they embody, although you can certainly find them on buildings that are both elegant and elaborate. You may find shingles and shakes of redwood, red and white cedar, or cypress, but western red cedar is the dominant species used throughout the United States. Both products display a tapered profile; however, shingles are sawn from a log, with two smooth surfaces, while shakes are split from the log, yielding a rough face. As a result, a bundle of shingles is much more uniform than a bundle of shakes, and shingles are also much thinner. Some shakes, called "split and resawn," are hand-split from the log and then the back face is cut smooth. Shingles and shakes are available in a range of sizes from 16 to 24 inches long, and the

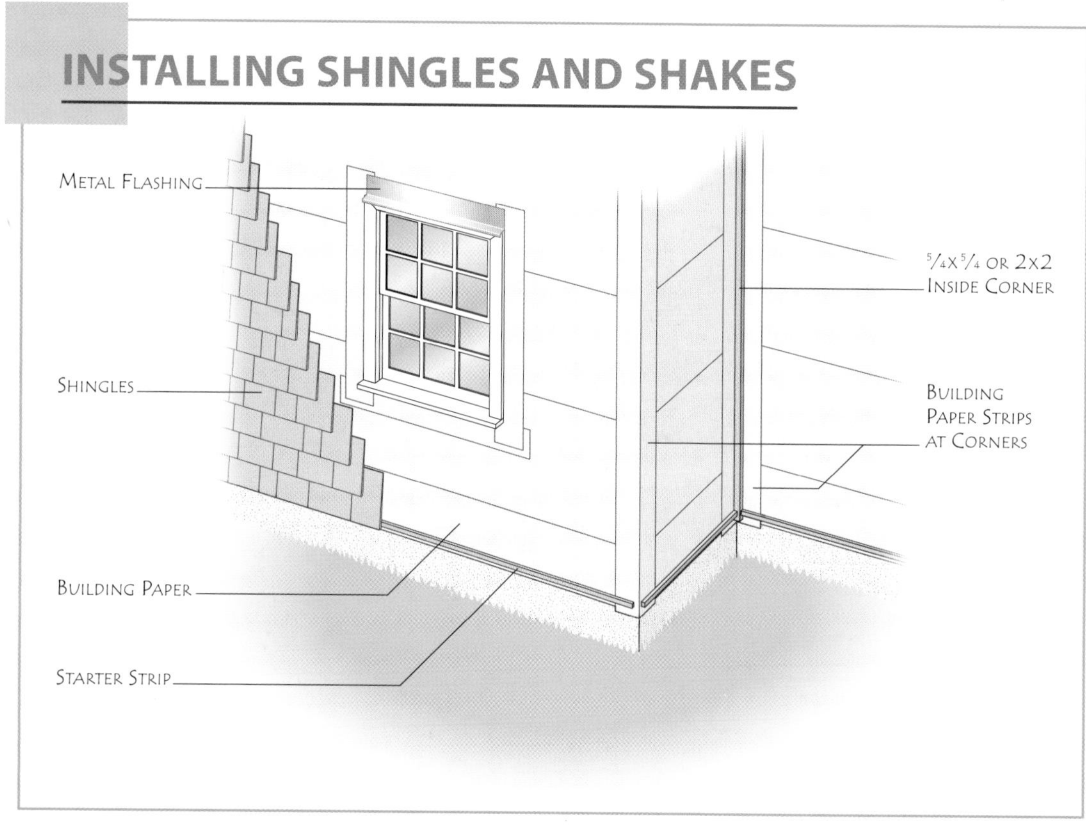

MOST SHINGLES are cut square, but the scallop design shown **above** is also popular. Fancy-cut shingles are best used as accents to clapboard. Diamond and arrow shapes are also available.

SMART TIP GOOD NAILING

A shingle or shake siding job involves driving many nails to hold the siding in place. Because the individual elements of the siding are so small, it would be impossible to fasten each to the wall framing. As a result, most of the nails will be driven into the wall sheathing, and it is important that the wall sheathing be a material that will provide a solid nailing surface—½-inch-thick plywood is best. If it is impossible to provide a solid nailing base, it is also acceptable to install horizontal furring strips, made from 1x3 or 1x4 lumber, to accept the shingle nails.

particular size chosen depends on the amount of each course that will be visible, which is called the "exposure" and can vary from 4 to 12 inches.

This type of siding provides the opportunity to customize the exterior of your home, as there are many variations of exposure and pattern that are available. They can be installed in either single or double courses, and in straight rows or staggered courses. In addition, some manufacturers offer shingles that are cut with decorative shapes along their bottom edges, and these can be used alone or in combination with other varieties of siding on distinct areas of the same building.

Inside corners are typically finished with corner posts that allow the installer to simply butt the shingles or shakes to them. Outside corners can be trimmed with corner boards, but they can also be "woven," a technique in which the installer alternates the outside edge overlap with each succeeding course.

Shingles and shakes are great options for a high-end siding job, but as you might expect, they are quite expensive to install. Not only is the raw material expensive, but also the labor involved in applying many individual pieces is significant. As the complexity of the shingle pattern grows, the more you can expect to pay.

SHAKES AND SHINGLES provide an appealing rustic finish. Shingles have smooth surfaces; shakes are split from a log and have a rough face.

PLYWOOD SIDING

PLYWOOD SIDING is constructed using the same process as construction-grade plywood. Alternating sheets of veneer are glued together with each oriented 90 degrees to the adjacent layers. The "show" face of the panel is usually a more expensive, and more decorative, grade and species of wood than the core—cedar, redwood, and cypress are the most frequent choices, but Douglas fir and southern pine are also used. Often the panels are milled to show a decorative pattern of grooves, and the face veneer can also be treated to yield a rough-sawn or rustic texture.

T 1-11. One of the most popular and most available varieties of plywood siding is called T 1-11, or Texture 1-11. T 1-11 is the American Plywood Association trade name for a style of panel with grooves spaced 4 or 8 inches on center down the length of the sheet. These panels have ship-lapped edges to minimize exposure of the panel core to the weather.

While the best results will be achieved when plywood siding is applied over a sheathed wall surface, if the siding panels are at least ⅝ inch thick, they can be nailed directly to the wall studs. It is extremely important to seal all panel edges before installing each sheet, and the entire job must be stained or painted soon after completion. Whenever two panels must be joined vertically, it is necessary to use a metal Z-channel flashing to ensure that water doesn't penetrate the joint between the sheets.

Plywood siding was widely used in low- and moderate-cost housing in the 1970s and '80s. In many cases, lack of proper installation and finishing caused splitting and delamination problems, and as a result some home builders started to use other materials. However, if properly installed, finished, and maintained, plywood siding can be an economical alternative to solid wood siding.

PLYWOOD SIDING is available in a number of designs, including T 1-11 panels, **above and below.** These panels contain precut grooves the full length of the panel.

VERTICAL BATTENS, below, add a nice architectural touch to plywood siding.

SMART TIP PLYWOOD AND CORNER BOARDS

When using plywood siding in combination with wood trim, the installer has the option of installing the inside and outside corner boards either before or after the panel stock. If the trim is to be applied after the siding, it is not as critical that every cut be perfect, because the boards will cover those joints. When the trim is installed before the siding panels, cuts must be neat and accurate, leaving a uniform gap of ⅛ inch between the parts. In either case, it is extremely important to caulk the joints to prevent moisture from getting to the panel core.

COMBINING SIDING TYPES is a common design practice. Here, plywood siding covers the second floor, while clapboard decorates the first floor.

Color Schemes

COLOR IS AN INTEGRAL ELEMENT in exterior design. Use it to emphasize architectural details, to express your own personality, or even to accent your prize-winning flower gardens.

Depending on the size and detail of your house, you could be choosing up to six colors to make details pop and seem three-dimensional. For this effect, a complex Victorian may require a different color for every trim detail, from shutters to door casings. A simple cottage may only need a base color and an accenting trim color.

To make trimwork stand out, consider using darker or lighter shades of the base color instead of changing color completely. Light colors will make a house seem larger, while dark colors will draw more attention to details.

It's true, your house is your canvas—but it's far from blank. When you look at your home's exterior, look at the big picture. Other elements, like brickwork and roof shingles, should influence your color palette. Use the bluish hues in your slate roof to choose similar colors for other details. Look at the landscape and houses surrounding yours for more inspiration. You might choose a creamy spring green to complement your flowering pink cherry blossoms or a robin's-egg blue that comes alive against your neighbor's sunny yellow siding.

COLOR SELECTION can set the tone of many house designs. Multiple complementary colors, **left,** work best on complex designs. A bold color for the siding that is offset by contrasting trimwork, **opposite top,** is a common design strategy. Picking colors that complement the landscape or nearby buildings, **opposite bottom,** helps the design blend with the surrounding area.

NON-WOOD SIDING

THERE ARE A NUMBER OF PRODUCTS on the market that are designed to look like wood clapboard, shakes, or shingles. Some are more successful at looking like wood than others. Most of these products are made of materials that require little or no maintenance.

Vinyl Siding

Vinyl siding is a product with broad appeal for those seeking to reduce the maintenance required on the exterior of their homes. It is available in a variety of styles, including clapboard, vertical, and shingle configurations, some with surface textures that suggest wood grain and others that are smooth. Like aluminum siding, vinyl comes with a factory finish that requires no painting. Systems include components for window, door, soffit, and corner-board trim, but it is also possible to combine vinyl siding with wood trim on doors and windows or to use aluminum trim. In any case, special J-channel molding is used to cover the cut ends of the siding pieces where they abut a piece of casing. End joints between adjacent panels must be overlapped by at least 1 inch.

This type of siding is engineered to allow seasonal movement. Pieces are fastened to the wall surface by nailing through slotted holes in the top edge of the siding, and it is important that the nails are not driven too tightly so the siding can expand and contract without cracking. The bottom edge of each piece hooks onto the next lower panel, locking the pieces together in a flexible joint.

Vinyl is suitable for both new and re-siding applications. When covering existing siding, it may be necessary to extend window and door trim to accommodate the additional depth of the siding. Vinyl siding is a flexible material, so it is important that the surface underneath is flat and straight to prevent a wavy appearance in the siding. This means that furring strips or shims might be required

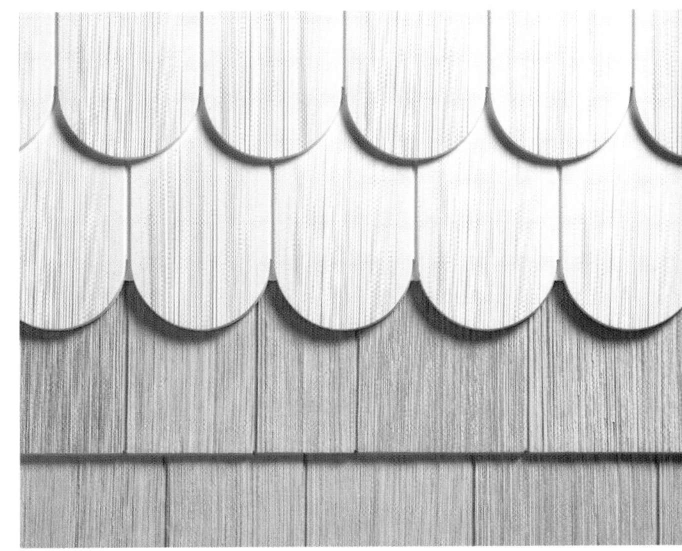

SMART TIP CLEANING VINYL SIDING

One of the challenges of maintaining vinyl siding is determining how to clean it without degrading or changing the surface of the material. One good approach is to use a long-handled soft brush that attaches to the end of a hose. If a more aggressive approach is required, try mixing regular laundry detergent with a powdered household cleanser and water. Avoid aggressive scrubbing with a tough-bristled brush and the use of abrasive cleaners because either approach could dull the factory finish of the siding and cause uneven streaking.

to build up low spots in the sidewalls before the vinyl installation. In some cases, it could also be necessary to remove the old siding before applying vinyl; any surface that is too flexible—like old vinyl or aluminum—will not properly support the new siding.

When considering vinyl as a siding material, it is important to note that it can develop certain problems. Factory finishes can fade with exposure to sunlight, and the material can also get brittle and crack as it ages. Cracks are impossible to repair in vinyl, so the only option is replacement of the damaged piece, and replacement parts usually will not match the existing siding due to inevitable color fading.

ALTHOUGH THEY LOOK LIKE WOOD, all of the houses shown here are finished with vinyl siding. The material is available in a variety of colors and trim pieces, **opposite top.** The siding can look like wood clapboard, **opposite bottom,** or plywood siding as shown on the second floor, **right.** Some manufacturers make vinyl panels with scallops or other designs, **above right.** Panels are available with a smooth finish or a simulated wood grain.

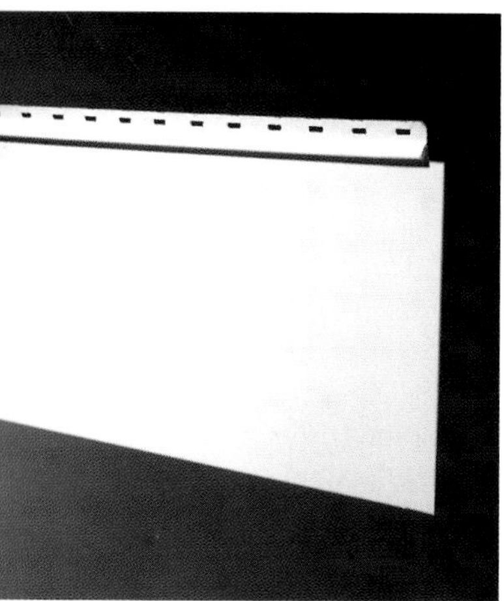

ALUMINUM SIDING offers a maintenance-free finish. Most manufacturers offer flat coil stock in a variety of colors that can be used on windows and door casings.

Aluminum Siding

Aluminum has long been sold as the "maintenance-free" siding. While this may be somewhat true, it may be an exaggeration to suggest that it is a carefree solution to the siding question. Aluminum siding is manufactured in sections that are meant to mimic the appearance of wood clapboard siding. Each section is normally two tiers high. The lower edge of each piece of siding must be hooked onto the upper edge of the previous course, while the upper edge is nailed to the wall studs through a series of slotted holes. Special J-channel molding is used at the junction of siding and trim to hide the cut ends of the siding pieces. Similarly, both outside corner post and inside corner stock are provided for those particular applications.

The use of aluminum for siding can also include the application of aluminum trim pieces as well. Moldings on windows and doors may be covered by flat aluminum stock that comes in coiled rolls. The installer shapes individual pieces of aluminum to fit the trim using shears and a sheet-metal brake. In addition, specialized trim for soffits, fascias, and rakes are manufactured in aluminum. These systems can be used as part of a complete aluminum siding job, or they can be used in conjunction with another siding material, often as a means of covering old, damaged trim.

Because aluminum has a factory-applied finish, it is sold as the siding that doesn't require painting, which is its primary attraction. But aluminum can develop other problems, such as dents and fading, that are difficult to repair. With changes in temperature, aluminum siding has been known to make "popping" and "cracking" noises as it expands and contracts. In addition, advocates of historic house preservation generally do not approve of aluminum siding because the installation often involves removing decorative trim items that could interfere with the aluminum trim.

Concrete Siding

CONCRETE HAS GROWN in popularity among designers and architects as they develop new uses for this material that has been a part of the building industry for years. Until recently, concrete was confined to foundations and retaining walls, but today's designers are discovering new uses for the material. Because it can be molded and formed into just about any shape, concrete is being used for countertops, interior walls, and fireplace mantels. When used as an exterior wall, concrete can be used to form unusual shapes and designs.

SMART TIP ALUMINUM SIDING SAFETY

Because aluminum siding is a metal product, it presents a particularly attractive target in a thunderstorm. To remove any hazard that its use might present, most building codes require that the siding be grounded to a water pipe or copper grounding stake. Special grounding clips allow the installer to connect a wire to both the stake and the siding panel.

SPECIAL J-CHANNELS hide the junction between siding panels and trimwork, such as window casings. Aluminum soffits, fascias, and rakes are also available.

Fiber-Cement Siding

For those who have already decided to apply some type of paint-grade siding, fiber-cement siding is well worth considering. Falling somewhere in cost between cedar and vinyl products, fiber-cement offers many advantages. This type of siding is made of a mixture of Portland cement, wood fiber, and sand; it is therefore a hybrid masonry/wood product. It is dimensionally stable and holds a painted finish better than solid wood siding. The most common type of fiber-cement siding is lap siding, which appears, when installed, like wood clapboard. Various widths are available, starting at 5¼ inches and running to 12 inches, offering a range of appearance. Other configurations, such as shingle-style and vertical panels are also offered.

Installing a fiber-cement siding job requires a set of techniques somewhat different from traditional woodworking skills, although some of these also apply. The material can be cut with carbide-tipped or abrasive saw blades or specialized shears. Circular saw cuts will always result in a considerable amount of nuisance dust, so it is extremely important that the installers wear proper dust masks and goggles for protection. It is hard to hand-drive nails through the siding, so a pneumatic nail gun is a necessity on this type of job. In addition, for maximum holding, nails must be driven so that the heads sit just against the surface of the panel, not below the surface.

Trim on a fiber-cement siding job can be treated in a variety of ways. Wood, aluminum, vinyl, and fiber-cement trim elements can all be used because no special channels are required at the junction of siding and casings or corner boards. When using fiber-cement trim elements, it is often necessary to build up the details with wood blocking because normal fiber-cement trim is only 7⁄16-inch thick.

FIBER-CEMENT SIDING, right, is made from Portland cement, wood fibers, and sand. It can be made to resemble wood siding, and like wood products, fiber-cement requires a painted finish.

TRIMWORK used on fiber-cement-sided houses, **opposite,** can be solid wood, vinyl, or fiber-cement components. The material is more difficult than wood to work, requiring carbide or abrasive saw blades.

Hardboard Siding

HARDBOARD SIDING is manufactured like hardboard trim stock: ground wood fiber is combined with preservatives and glue, and then pressed into molds and heated. The fabrication process allows the material to be formed into a variety of shapes, including tapered clapboard-like pieces as well as panels of different sizes. Hardboard is extremely sensitive to moisture, so because it will be exposed to the weather, extra care must be taken to prevent water from contaminating the core. Unless it's properly sealed, changes in humidity can cause the product to expand along its length, resulting in buckling.

While most of these products come with a factory-applied primer, it is extremely important to seal all field-cuts before installation. In addition, whenever possible, protect the ends of each piece from direct exposure to rain by using metal H-channel trim at butt joints and rabbeted corner boards at outside corners. It is also important to leave a ⅛-inch gap between adjacent pieces at butt-joints and trim, and to carefully caulk these joints. Use galvanized siding nails for fastening, and drive the nail heads flush with the board surface. If a nail head breaks the surface of a piece, moisture can enter the core and cause it to swell or blister.

STUCCO

STUCCO IS A MIXTURE of sand and Portland cement that is applied to exterior walls. On a wood frame wall, first a moisture-resistant membrane is applied to the sheathing, followed by an expanded metal or wire lath. Next, three coats of stucco are applied: the first coat is called a scratch coat; the second is called a brown coat; and the last is called a finish coat. The first two coats are a mixture of Portland and masonry cement and sand in different proportions. The finish coat contains white cement, lime, and sand, and it can be mixed with pigment to yield various colors. It can also be smoothed with a trowel, swirled with a float, or dabbed with a brush to create a range of textures. Overall thickness of a traditional stucco application is approximately ⅞ inch. When stucco is applied to a brick or cement-block wall, only a brown coat and finish coat are required.

There are also stucco finishes called one-coat or thin-coat applications. In fact, these systems consist of a thick fiberglass-reinforced base coat and then a finish coat that

A STUCCO FINISH, below, provides a distinctive look that other siding materials cannot duplicate. Stucco can be used to create decorative elements, as well as solid coverage.

can be either a cement-based or acrylic-based material. One-coat stucco can be applied with less curing time between coats than traditional stucco, but the material is not as resistant to impact as the three-coat application. It also does not have the longevity of traditional stucco, with an expected life about one half that of the traditional system. In many cases, wood trim is used in conjunction with stucco siding, but cast concrete or stone trim details are also compatible treatments.

Almost all stucco surfaces will need repair as they age. As a house settles or materials expand and contract seasonally, the stucco remains a relatively inflexible shell, and the resulting tension can cause cracks. Fortunately, it is possible to repair almost any crack that appears in a stucco surface. Small cracks or holes can sometimes be successfully repaired by mixing pigment into the patching material. However, when a large hole or crack is involved, it's rarely possible to make the patch invisible. As a result, it is usually necessary to paint the siding to restore the stucco to a like-new appearance.

WOOD TRIMWORK, top, is often used with stucco siding.

STUCCO provides the ability to cover curves and other odd shapes, **above.**

BRICK appeared as the siding material of choice on many early American housing styles, such as Federal and Georgian.

BRICK

OF ALL SIDING MATERIALS, brick veneer is clearly the most durable. However, even this type of siding may require periodic repair or maintenance. Brick can be applied to an entire wall or just a section of a wall, with some other siding material used to finish the balance. It is available in a wide range of colors and textures to create a variety of design options, from formal to rustic.

In new construction, the block or poured-concrete foundation should be constructed so that it provides an integral 4-inch-wide ledge to support the weight of the brick. For an existing foundation that doesn't have such a ledge, a stainless-steel angle can be bolted to the foundation to support the material. In these situations, the height of the brick is limited to 12 to 14 feet. For window and door openings, the most common approach is to use a lintel, formed from steel angle, to carry the weight of the brick above; it is also possible to build an arch without steel to span a wall opening.

In many ways, a brick veneer installation is a structure independent of the building it surrounds. So it is important to install brick ties to connect the siding to the wall structure. There are several styles of brick ties available, but for residential construction, ties formed from corrugated metal are the most common. For wood frame walls, ties are nailed to the studs (one per stud every 6 or 7 courses), and on concrete-block walls, the ties are installed in the mortar joints as the

SMART TIP BRICK MAINTENANCE

While brick presents the image of a tough, impermeable facade for a building, the truth is that brick is a porous material, most often composed of clay. As a result, bricks can absorb water and are susceptible to damage from periodic freezing and thawing in winter. To preserve the brick, apply a clear, water-repellent sealer to keep any moisture from penetrating its surface.

wall is built. As the brick veneer is installed, the free ends of the ties are fit into the mortar joints. Weep holes, to allow moisture to escape from behind the brick, and expansion joints, to prevent cracking, must also be designed into a brick siding job.

Maintenance for brick siding generally involves re-pointing the mortar joints. Severe weather, particularly the freeze-and-thaw cycle, can cause the mortar between the bricks to crack. Eventually the joints can deteriorate, weakening the bond and creating the opportunity for leaks to develop. The solution to this situation is to rake out the old, brittle material, and use a special tuck-pointing trowel to install new mortar.

FOR A STATELY DESIGN, brick is often the material of choice as it complements most trimwork treatments. Note the frieze and pediment below.

CHAPTER 8

TOOLS AND MATERIALS

ANY TYPE OF CARPENTRY WORK inevitably involves tool use. Sometimes these are the most basic hand tools, implements that haven't changed much for hundreds of years, and at other times they can be elaborate new models of machines designed to work with materials that didn't even exist until very recently. This chapter examines the group of tools that goes beyond those you might find in a typical home toolbox.

In addition to selecting the right tools, you will also need to select the right material for the job. While most people automatically think of solid wood when they think of exterior trimwork, there are a variety of other products available, including engineered-wood products, recycled materials, and plastics. They all have their own strengths and weaknesses. Becoming familiar with the products will help you select the best material for your job.

BASIC TOOLS

THERE IS NO REASON to sacrifice your retirement savings to amass a collection of tools you'll never use. But if you are interested in becoming proficient in the basic maintenance and repair jobs that will arise for any homeowner, a modest collection of tools will repay your investment many times over. Here's a look at some of the tools you may not already own but will come in handy when making repairs on exterior trimwork.

Squares

The concept of "square" is basic in carpentry. Simply stated, it means that two surfaces are perfectly perpendicular, and the tool used to test this is appropriately known as a square. Squares come in a variety of configurations, each designed for a particular use. For exterior trim you will find these varieties most useful.

Framing Square. A framing square is made of steel or aluminum with legs of 16 and 24 inches. In addition to the standard inch measurements on each blade, a framing square always has a chart that you can use to determine the cut angles for rafters of any roof pitch. Use this tool to layout wall studs and also to test that openings or panels are square. The long blade is also very valuable as a straight edge.

Try-Square. A try-square is a small square with a 6 or 8 inch blade that has a fixed body or "stock." This tool is handy for marking cut-lines on solid wood material, to test the accuracy of a cut, or to check that the edge of a board is square to the face. A good quality try-square is guaranteed to conform to fine tolerances of accuracy.

Speed Square. A speed square is designed to be used to layout simple rafter cuts, but it has another use as a crosscutting guide

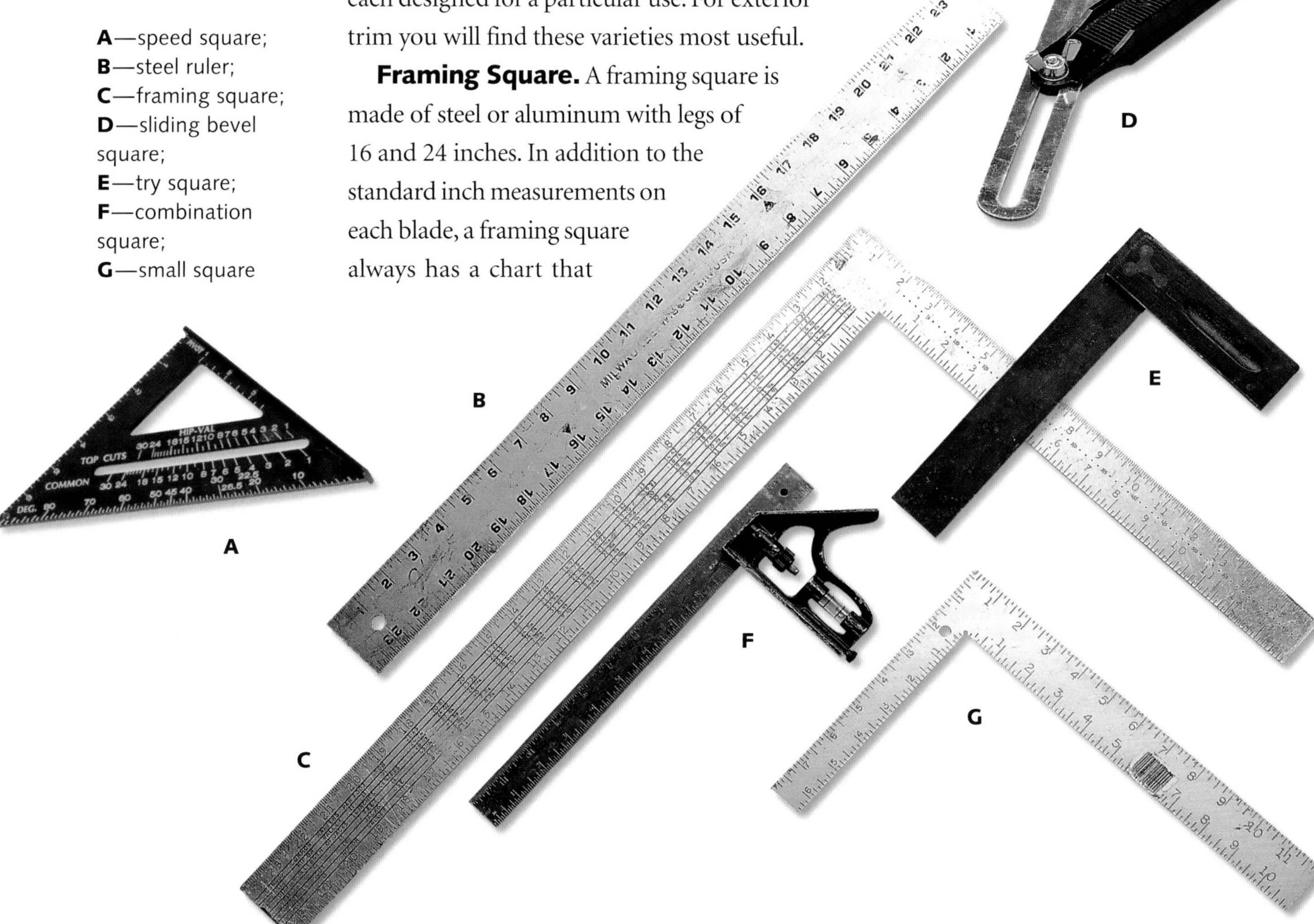

A—speed square;
B—steel ruler;
C—framing square;
D—sliding bevel square;
E—try square;
F—combination square;
G—small square

Safety Checklist

- GOGGLES
- DUST MASK
- RESPIRATOR
- EAR PROTECTION
- LEATHER WORK GLOVES
- VINYL OR NITRILE GLOVES
- FIRST-AID KIT

EVERY CARPENTER knows that a speed square is a good tool to keep handy because it can double as a saw guide.

for the circular or jig saw. Hold or clamp the square against the edge of a narrow board and run the saw foot along the blade to make a square cut.

Combination Square. This tool has a milled edge on the body that sits at 45 degrees to the blade for testing miter cuts. The body can slide along the graduated blade and lock in place at different settings so that you can use it as a depth or marking gauge. Most models include a steel scriber and a small level vial on the body.

Levels

Plumb and level are concepts that are used in all forms of carpentry, both structural and decorative. Something is considered level when it is perfectly parallel with the ground with no slope. Plumb describes the condition of being perfectly vertical. Level and plumb lines are always perpendicular. You can test these qualities with a spirit level. A level contains two or three arched vials filled with liquid with a small bubble inside. To test whether a surface is plumb or level, hold the tool firmly against the part and check that the bubble is perfectly centered between the gauge marks. Levels are available in a variety of sizes, but for trim work you will find three sizes most useful—a 9-inch torpedo level and 24- and 48-inch models. Good quality tools are offered with either wood or metal bodies.

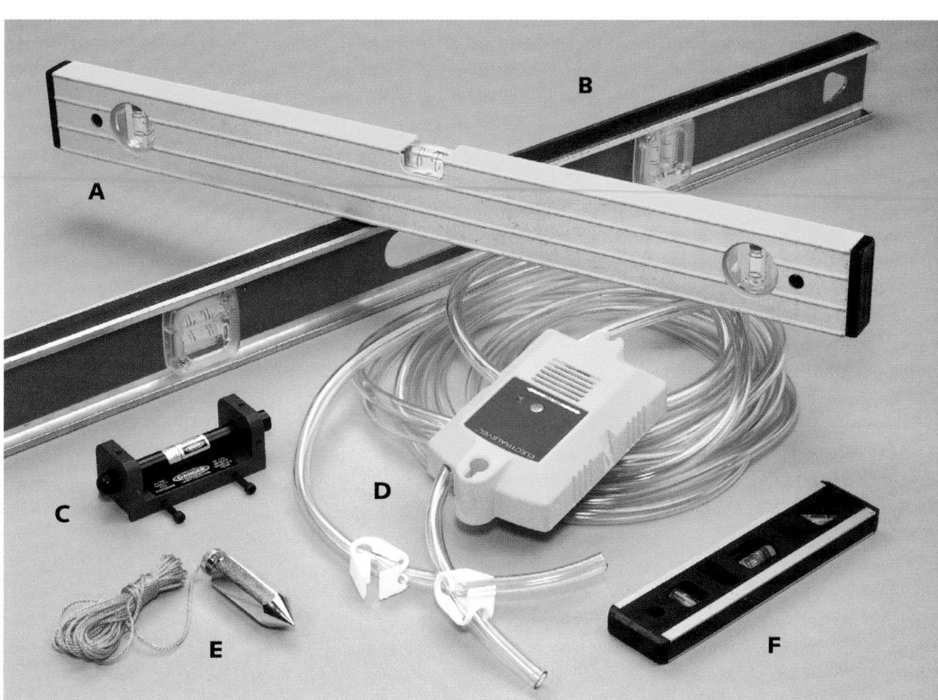

A—2-ft. spirit level; **B**—4-ft. spirit level; **C**—laser level; **D**—water level with electronic sensor; **E**—plumb bob; **F**—9-in. spirit level

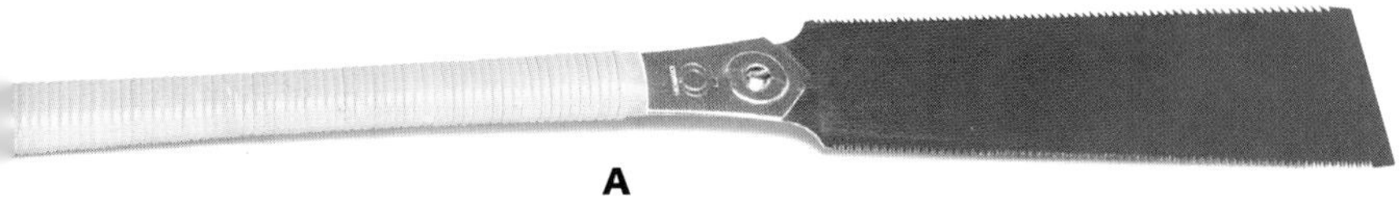

A—Japanese Ryoba saw; B—back saw; C—coping saw; D—miter box; E—adjustable hand miter saw; F—block plane

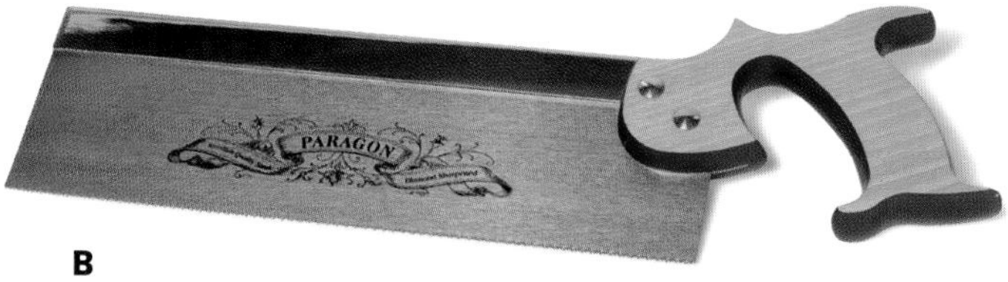

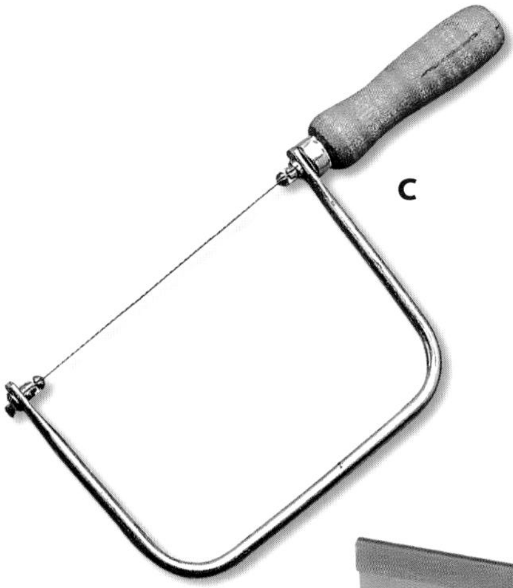

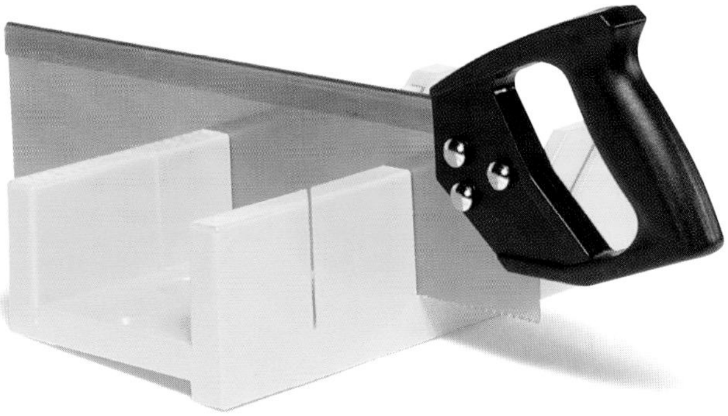

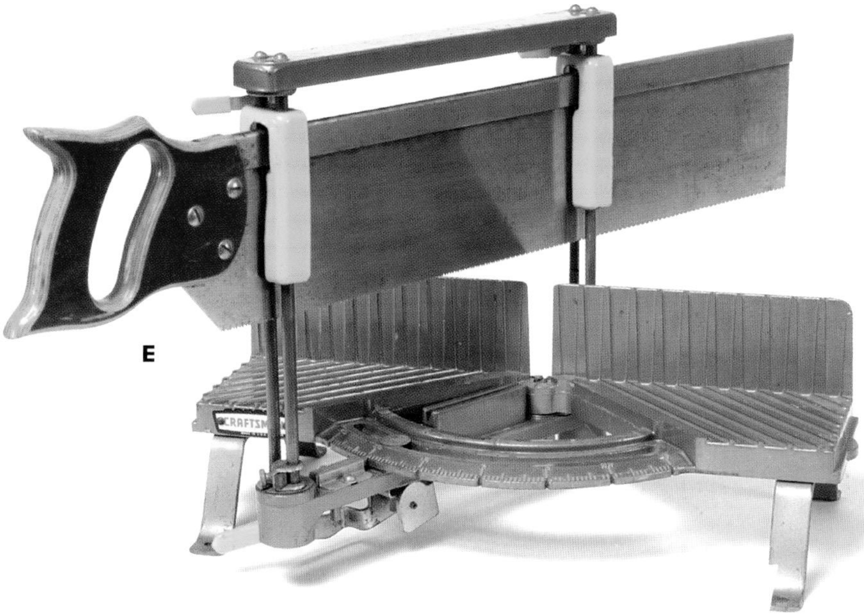

Saws

Hand Saws. If you need to make a simple cut, or when a power saw would be awkward or dangerous to use, a traditional hand saw is the tool of choice. There are a number of types from which to choose. For general use, look for a compact tool with a blade about 15 inches long and a cutting edge with 8 teeth per inch. When using the saw, position yourself so that you can take long, straight strokes, with your arm and shoulder in line with the blade. If the saw is properly sharpened, you will not need to force the blade, but simply guide it back and forth, allowing the weight of the blade to determine the rate of cut.

Coping Saws. A coping saw is designed to be used when making intricate cuts for fitted molding joints at inside corners. The saw consists of a handle attached to a C-shaped frame. A thin blade is stretched between the ends of the frame. The open configuration allows the user to make sharp turns with the blade to follow complex molding shapes. Because the blades are so thin, install them to cut on the pull-stroke to avoid breaking them.

Block Planes

Planes are one of the tools most often associated with carpentry work, and there is good reason for this notion. A plane is the premier tool for rough or final fitting of trim boards or shaving a door or window for smooth operation. You can also use a plane to flatten

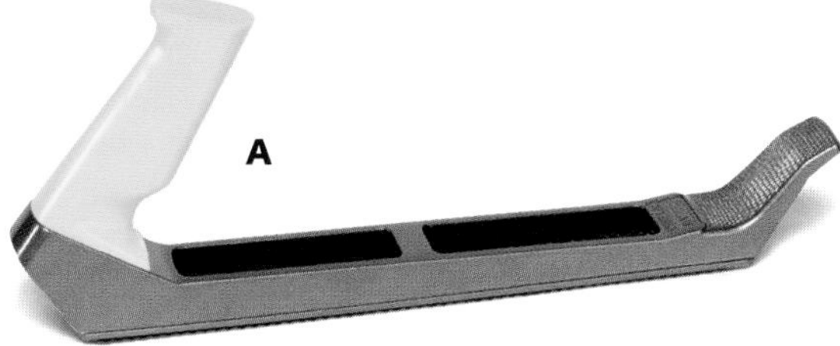

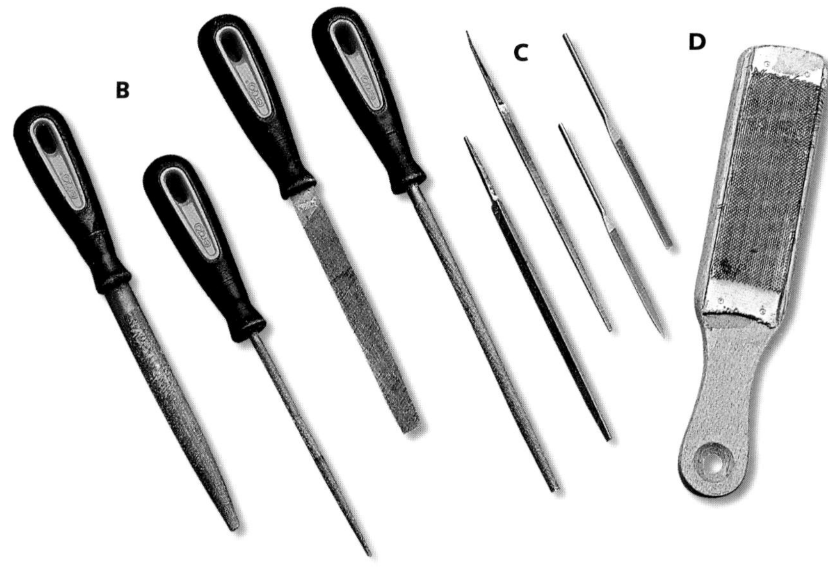

A—Surform tool; B—large files; C—mini-files; D—file card

twisted stock or reduce the overall thickness of a board. While there are specialty planes for almost any particular task, a beginner will find a block plane is a good general-purpose choice. A block plane is about 6 inches long, with a cutting iron about 1½ inches wide. The iron is mounted at a low angle with the bevel facing up. This design makes it ideal for trimming the end grain of a board, but you can use it for edge or face planing as well.

Files and Rasps

One of the more challenging jobs in trim carpentry involves fitting a wooden part to an uneven surface such as brick, stone, stucco, or intricate molding. In these situations you will find that a variety of tools are required to achieve a tight joint. Often the most direct approach is to use a rough abrasive tool like a Surform or rasp to shape the edge. A Surform has an expanded metal blade that is held in a frame so that it can be easily manipulated. These come in a variety of shapes and sizes so you can select the most appropriate for your task.

Rasps also come in a variety of shapes, sizes, and tooth configurations. If you want to select only one tool for your kit, a half-round variety is probably the most useful.

Cordless Drill/Driver

Many power tools are now available in cordless models, but the one tool that clearly excels as a cordless tool is the combination drill/driver. Models are available with ratings from 7.2V to 24V, but as a non-professional, a drill with a 12V or 14.4V battery will provide plenty of power. All cordless drill/drivers are equipped with keyless chucks and most have adjustable clutch settings that allow you to set the torque to high for drilling in wood or low for driving small screws. Select a model with a ⅜- or ½-inch chuck for maximum flexibility in the choice of bits you can use.

USE A CORDLESS DRILL/DRIVER, below, to drill pilot holes for screws, drive screws, and remove screws in trimwork.

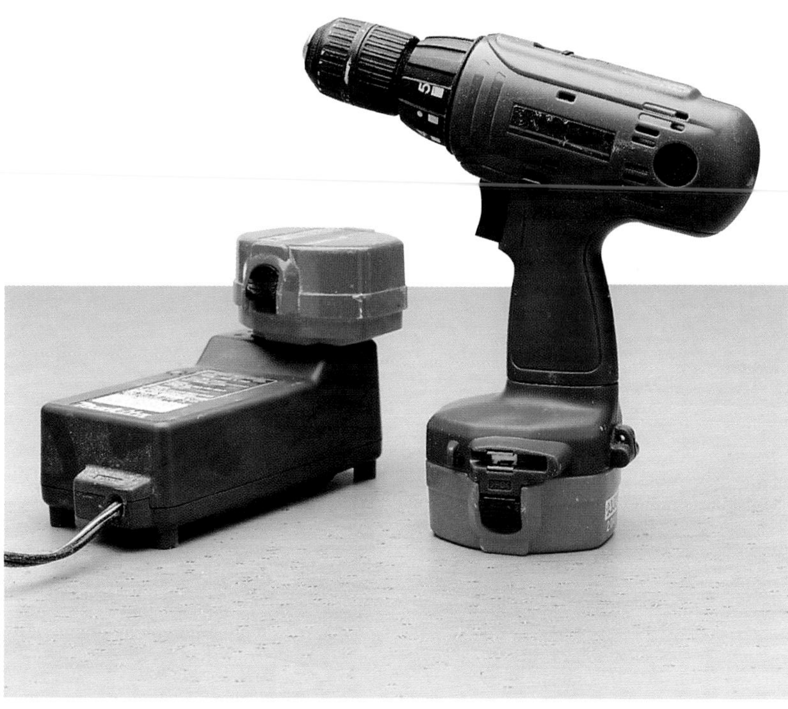

THE FINISHING AND REPAIR of trimwork usually involves some sanding. The random-orbital sander, **top,** is a finish sander that leaves a smooth surface for finishing chores. Sheet sanders, **center,** are designed to sand with the grain of the wood. The belt sander, **above,** removes material quickly.

Sanding and Paint Removal

Sanding is an unpleasant but necessary part of most projects that involve wooden trim. But the job can be made much more efficient by the choice of the right sander.

Random Orbital Sanders. A random orbital sander is a finishing sander with a disc-shaped pad. The sanding pad turns on an eccentric spindle so that it creates tiny swirl marks on the wood surface. This type of sander has the ability to remove stock quite rapidly and still provide an excellent finish. Look for a sander with a 5-inch-diameter pad, because that size disc is the most widely available. Some sanders have built-in dust collection systems that require sanding discs with holes punched through them. Make sure that any discs you buy match the hole pattern on the sander pad.

Other Sanders. Orbital sheet sanders require square or rectangular pads. They are offered in ¼- and ½-sheet sizes. They are generally the least expensive options for power sanding.

Belt Sanders. These tools are designed to remove a lot of wood quickly, but they can also get out of control easily and cause some damage. Some pros use belt sanders for exterior trimwork, but for the average homeowner, belt sanders are difficult to handle on vertical surfaces.

Heat Guns. A heat gun can be an extremely valuable tool when you need to strip off old paint or remove old window glazing. Look for a model with a variable or two-speed switch so you can control the amount of heat being directed onto the work surface. Many of these guns can generate temperatures in excess of 1,000 degrees F, so use caution to prevent charring a wood surface or setting fire to a combustible material.

Abrasives

Abrasives play an important role in preparing new trim to accept a finish, and they are equally important when refinishing and repairing old trim. Although new lumber and millwork appear to be smooth, most often these pieces have mill marks and scratches that do not become apparent until a finish is applied. It's a good practice to sand the exposed surfaces of these parts, before priming, to yield a smooth base for the finish. If you're using drying filler for nailholes or repairs, it's best to slightly overfill each hole to allow for shrinkage. When the filler is dry, sand it flat. In addition, many primers leave a slightly rough surface that requires light sanding before applying a finish coat of paint. Old, weathered trim frequently needs some abrasive treatment, because paint can crack, peel, and chip off, leaving a rough, unsightly surface.

Abrasive Products. There are a good number of abrasive products to fill these needs, from simple sandpaper to specialized abrasive wheels. The standard size for sandpaper sheets is 9 × 11 inches, but you can also find ¼- and ½-sheet sizes that will fit various vibrating sanders. Belts in assorted sizes and grits are sold for portable belt sanders. Discs in 5- and 6-inch diameters are available for random orbital sanders; these are offered with self-adhesive and hook-and-loop backs to match whatever type of pad the sander has—some discs have holes for machines with dust collection. The most popular abrasive grit for these products is aluminum oxide; it is a long lasting material with an aggressive rate of cut.

Wheels of varied materials and diameters are designed to be mounted in a portable drill. Wire, Scotch-Brite, and flap-wheels are all handy for stripping old paint. When using any of these products, it is important that you wear a dust mask and eye protection. And if your house was built before 1979, the old paint could contain lead, so special precautions might be necessary. DIY lead test kits are available at home centers and hardware stores.

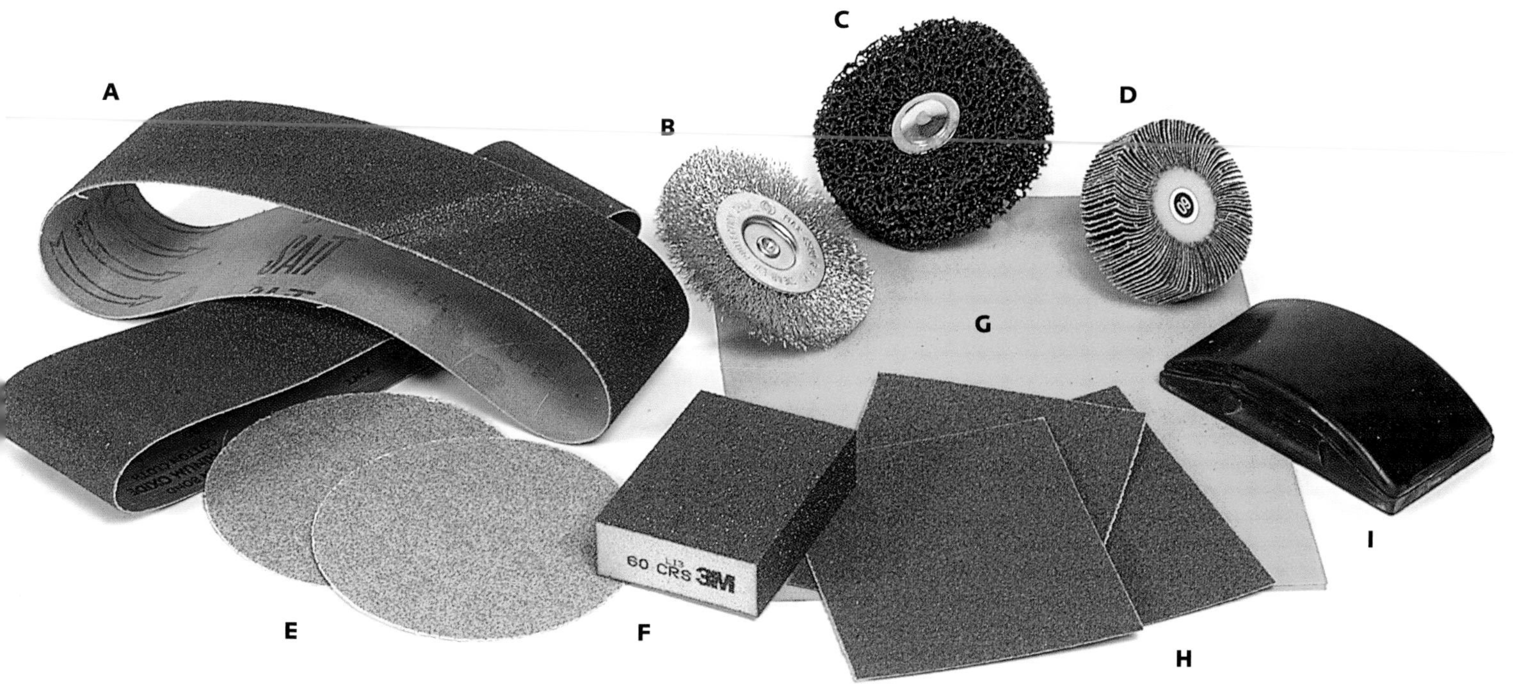

A—aluminum oxide sanding belts; **B**—4-in. wire wheel; **C**—4-in. "Scotch-Brite" paint and rust stripper; **D**—3-in. flap wheel; **E**—5-in. dia. self-adhesive sanding discs; **F**—sanding sponge; **G**—9- x 11-in. sandpaper; **H**—4½- x 5½-in. palm sanding sheets; **I**—rubber sanding block

POWER CUTTING TOOLS

Circular Saws

A portable circular saw is one of the most useful and versatile tools for the home carpenter. This is truly the workhorse of the toolbox, used to cut materials including plywood panels, two-by framing lumber, and pine trim. It is the tool of choice for both ripping and crosscutting lumber and it will accept a variety of blades for cutting different materials efficiently. Saws come in a variety of sizes, rated by the diameter of the saw blade, but for general use a $7\frac{1}{4}$-inch model is the most popular. These saws can easily cut through $1\frac{1}{2}$-inch-thick framing lumber with the blade set at either 90 or 45 degrees.

Some saw models are provided with an electronic brake that stops the blade when you release the trigger, and this is a great option for increased safety. If it does not come with the saw, you should purchase an accessory rip guide for cutting strips of uniform width from wide stock. A 40-tooth combination blade is a good choice for general use.

Jig Saws

When a project calls for producing intricate shapes or any curved cuts, a jig saw is the tool for the job. These accept a wide variety of blades for rough and finish cutting of wood as well as plastics and metal. Most models have an adjustable base for bevel cuts and a

CIRCULAR SAWS, top, are the most reached for power cutting tool on most job sites. Use jig saws, **center,** to make odd-shaped cuts, such as when repairing fancy gingerbread trim. Miter saws, **left,** make precise angle cuts.

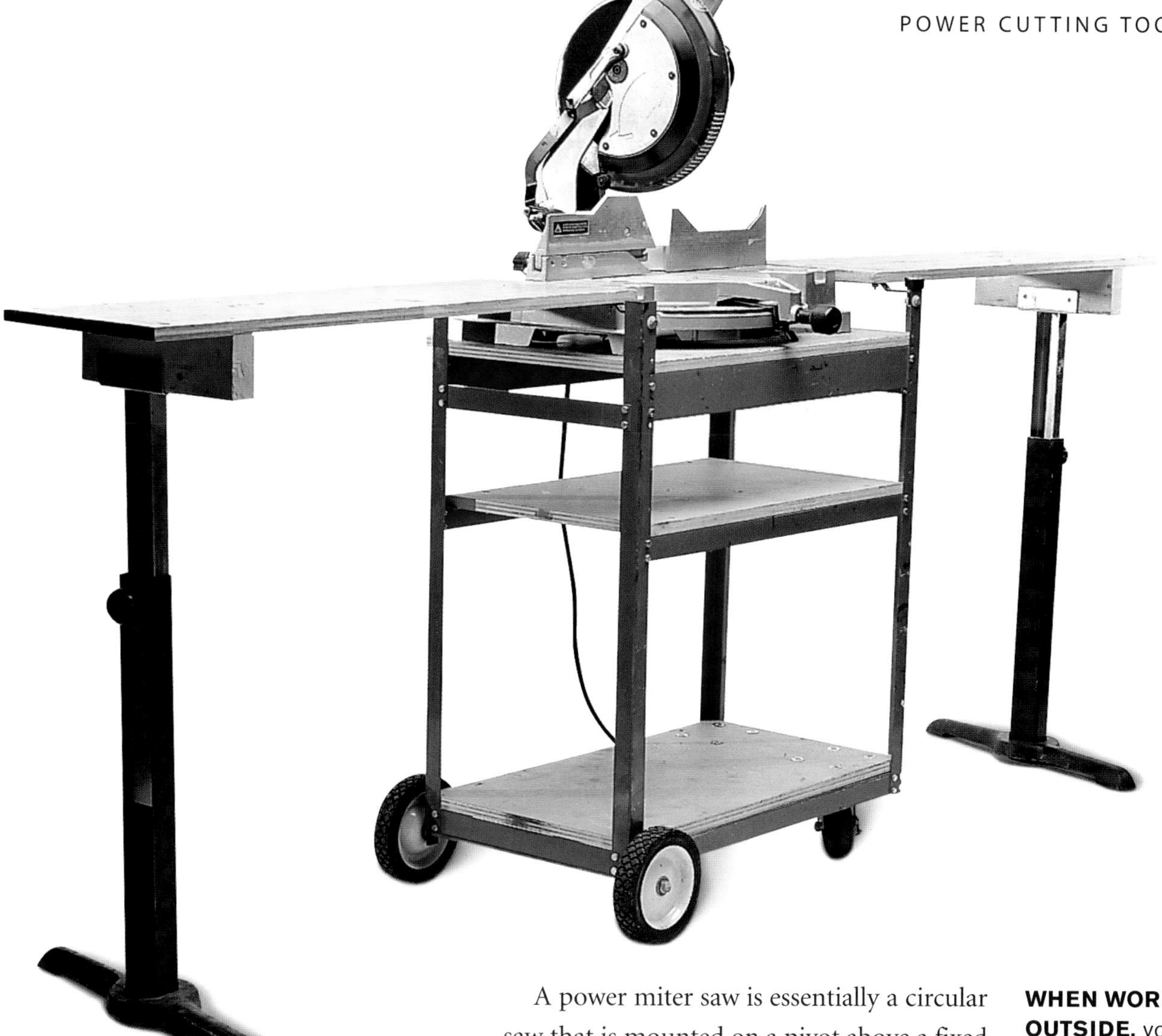

switch to allow the blade to move in either an orbital motion for wood or a reciprocal motion for plastic or metal.

Miter Saws

Miter saws range in complexity from the simplest wooden or plastic miter box with a hand saw that may cost $30 to elaborate sliding compound miter saws that can cost over $600. The saw you choose will depend on the nature and size of your job. If your project only includes a few simple 90- and 45-degree cuts, any saw will do. But for moldings that involve odd angles or compound miters, a tool with more adjustments will be required.

A power miter saw is essentially a circular saw that is mounted on a pivot above a fixed table. The motor and blade can swivel from side to side to cut a desired angle. Most saws have preset detents at 90, 45, and 22.5 degrees—the most frequently used settings. A compound miter saw has the added capability for the blade to tip to one side to cut a bevel angle in addition to the miter. A sliding compound miter saw adds another feature to the mix by providing guide rails that allow the blade to be pulled through the cut, toward the operator. Sliding saws enable you to crosscut wide stock, cut compound angles with a molding held flat on the saw table, and cut grooves or tenon joints by limiting the depth of cut with a stop. Power miter saws are rated by the diameter of the saw blade with most models in the 8- to 12-inch range.

WHEN WORKING OUTSIDE, you will need a workstation for your miter saw. You can buy one or make your own. Because you will be working with long lengths, be sure to support the wood.

Bench-Top Table Saws

A lightweight, bench-top table saw can be very practical on any trim job. A wide variety of 8- and 10-inch saws are available and these have become very popular as inexpensive alternatives to a free-standing contractor saw. These saws usually provide a rip fence and miter gauge as standard equipment, and they have a tilting arbor for bevel cuts. You should not expect that a bench-top saw will be the equivalent of a floor-model saw when it comes to accuracy or power, but for light-duty use they can do a great job. By necessity, these saws have relatively small motors, so it is important that you always use a thin-kerf saw blade for maximum efficiency.

BENCH-TOP TABLE SAWS, above, come in handy when it is time to rip lumber to size or cut a panel.

ROUTERS, below, allow you to shape wood so that you can create custom molding profiles or cut decorative grooves or flutes.

Because these saws are intentionally lightweight, always clamp or bolt the saw to a heavy worktable before making any cuts. You should also double-check the rip fence setting at both the front and back of the blade because these accessories are notorious for not automatically locking parallel with the blade.

Routers/Router Tables

A portable router will give you the ability to duplicate a wide range of molding profiles in addition to cutting grooves or flutes, and shaping the edges of boards and panels. Cutting bits are offered in a vast array of profiles and sizes, so you can usually count on finding one to fit your job requirements. Routers are rated by motor size and by the size of the shaft of the bit that the collet, or tool holder, will accept. For light-duty home use, look for a tool with a rating of 1½ or 1¾ hp with a ¼-inch collet.

A basic router will have a fixed base that requires you to set the depth of cut by adjusting a locking ring on the base. You need to adjust the depth of cut before turning on the tool. There are also models that feature a plunge base that allows you to lower a spinning bit into the work surface. If your router does not come with an accessory edge guide, you should definitely purchase one.

When you encounter a job that requires you to cut profiles on narrow or short stock, or just mill a lot of material, a router table is worth consideration. This accessory holds the router, upside down, in a fixed base that allows you to push the work past the spinning bit, rather than moving the router across the work piece. Because this configuration exposes the cutting bit, you need to take extra precautions for safety. Always clamp a fence to the table so that no more than one

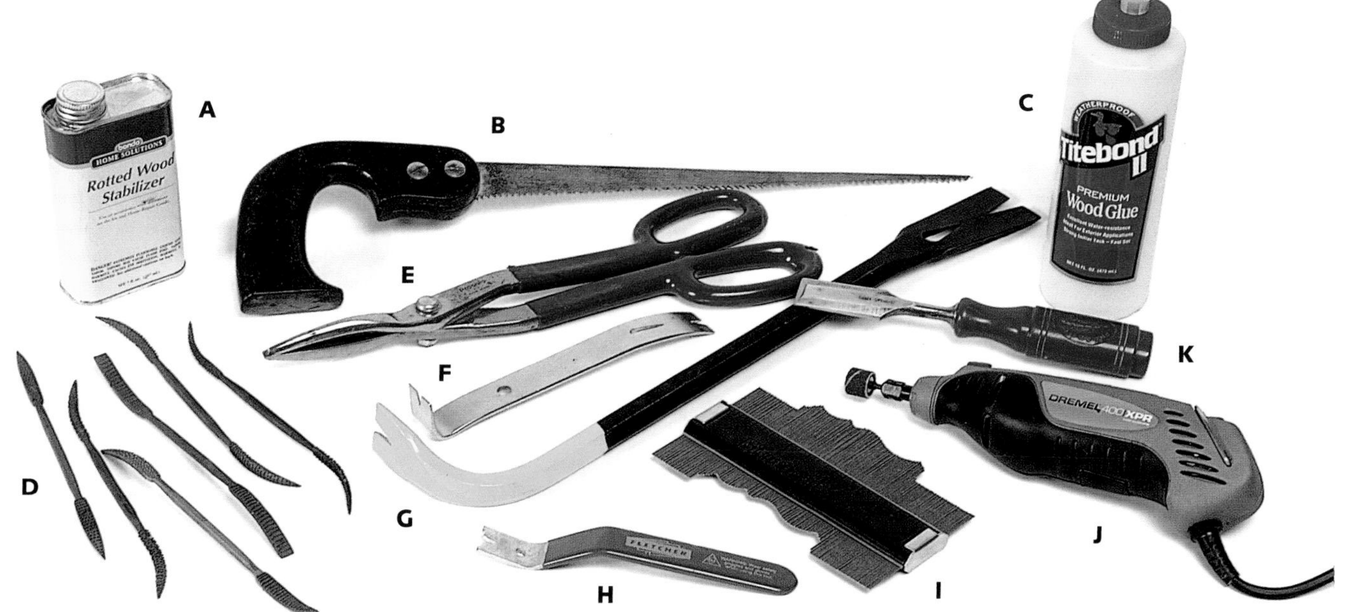

A—wood stabilizer; B—keyhole saw; C—waterproof glue; D—riffler set; E—metal shears; F—small pry bar; G—wrecking bar; H—glazing point tool; I—profile gauge; J—rotary tool; K—old chisel;

half of the bit is exposed. Whenever possible, use hold-down fixtures and guards to keep the work from kicking back and to keep your hands away from the cutting edge. When you shape small parts, push sticks are mandatory.

RESTORATION TOOLS

IF YOU PLAN TO GET INVOLVED in some restoration work, it pays to equip yourself with some tools to make the job as easy as possible. Of course, many of theses tools are also useful for general repair, but they are particularly handy for restoration work.

Before starting any demolition, it's best to record the existing profiles of any molding you're trying to restore. A *profile gauge* is extremely handy—just press the fingers against the molding to get an exact map of the shape.

For removing damaged material, it's great to have an *old chisel* and two sizes of *wrecking bars* at hand. An old chisel will allow you to chop into areas that might contain a stray nail without worrying about the tool's delicate edge. The wrecking bars provide leverage to remove either small or large pieces of trim.

A *keyhole saw* has a long, pointed blade that can reach into tight spots.

When a job requires you to replace a pane of window glass, a *glazing point tool* can make the job much safer than if you use a chisel or screwdriver. The tool has an end that is milled to match the shape of a glazing point, so you can press it into the edge of a window sash.

Chemical *wood stabilizer* is a solution you can apply to harden and stabilize the rotten edges of damaged trim before beginning a restoration.

Metal shears or *tin snips* are the tool to use for cutting aluminum or galvanized flashing stock to size.

Waterproof wood glue is an absolute necessity for exterior trim repair. While you could rely on mechanical fasteners, such as nails and screws, to hold a patch in place, glue provides a bond that is actually stronger than the wood fiber.

Once a patch or filler is set in place, you may need to shape it to match the original molding profile. *Rifflers,* small rasps in various shapes, and a *Dremel,* or other rotary tool, can be used to carve either resin or wood to any shape you need.

SELECT PINE, above left, has less knots than common-grade pine, resulting in a better finish.

SOLID WOOD TRIMWORK, below, provides the most possibilities when choosing a finish.

TRIMWORK MATERIALS

ONCE THE DESIGN DETAILS FOR YOUR TRIM are settled, it's time to determine the materials for the job. This is one of those places where you have a wide range of choices, and it may seem that there are so many options that there is no clear winner in the selection lottery. But if you become familiar with the attributes of each material, and weigh the comparative costs, the decision will be much simpler. Take advantage of your available resources. It's always a good idea to consult with your contractor and building materials supplier so that you can benefit from their professional experience and familiarity with various resources.

Because one of the main functions of trim is to present a particular style and appearance, it follows that the materials used should make it easy to maintain the look you want. This means that the finish that will be applied to the trim has a lot to do with the best choice of materials. While any of these lumber species provide some resistance to rot, those varieties with the highest resin content will last the longest, especially in locations with challenging weather conditions. The least expensive lumber variety will generally be pressure treated, followed, in order of increasing cost, by pine, Douglas fir, cedar, cypress, and redwood. You could also find that some varieties of lumber are not easy to find in all locations, because some types of trees only grow in particular climates and are not always shipped around the country. To further complicate matters, redwood, which is considered the premium material, is in limited supply due to the slow growth and limited supply of the trees. Sustainable forestry practices are now being used to ensure the future availability of the species. If the design plan calls for a clear or semitransparent stained finish, you generally want the trim to be one of the solid wood species. But, for a painted or opaque stained finish, the material universe is much wider, including solid wood, engineered wood products, plastic, and fiber-cement products.

Solid Wood Trim

Solid wood has long been the premium trim material. It is readily available, easy to cut and install, accepts any type of finish, and the subtle but distinct wood grain is attractive and elegant. And for many people, the fact that wood is a natural material is the definitive point in its favor. Wood trim works well with any type of siding, including wood, masonry, stucco, fiber-cement, vinyl, and aluminum; and you can choose trim details that match the siding material or provide dramatic contrast.

Because most exterior trim elements are exposed to extremes of weather and are also subject to insect infestation, it is important to use a species that provides some resistance to these elements. Lumber varieties with high natural resin content are the best choices for this use, and among these, pine, Douglas fir, redwood, western red cedar, and cypress are popular choices. In addition, pressure-treated lumber, mostly southern yellow pine, provides resistance to weathering as a result of being treated with a chemical solution.

Solid wood trim elements are most often constructed from lumber that is sold in standard sizes from 1×2 to 1×12. These nominal sizes are larger than the actual dimensions of the finished boards. Some architectural details, like corner boards and friezes, use stock that is referred to as 5⁄4 lumber. This classification refers to the thickness of a board in 1⁄4-inch increments before the rough lumber is planed to finished dimension. While the actual thickness of lumber can vary from species to species, in most cases 5⁄4 stock will be 1 1⁄8 inches thick.

When considering different solid lumber species for exterior trim, it's best to only consider stock that is free from knots and other major defects. Even if the trim is painted and the knots sealed with a suitable primer, they will eventually bleed through the finish, ruining an otherwise beautiful job. Suitable grades of pine and Douglas fir will be sold as "select" stock; cedar and cypress lumber are sold as "clear" grade. Redwood lumber has its own system of grading, with the highest grades called "clear all heart" and "heart B."

WHEN SELECTING A TRIM MATERIAL, it pays to pick the best material possible. Your work will last longer and require less maintenance.

Pressure-Treated Lumber. While pressure-treated stock is a possible choice for exterior trim, it does have some features that make it more challenging to install and less likely to perform well. The variety of lumber most often used is southern yellow pine, which is very heavy and has a coarse-grained texture. In addition, it's pretty rare to find stock that is flat and straight—qualities that are extremely important when applying trim. And because the lumber is usually delivered with very high moisture content, due to the preservative process, it cannot be painted until it has weathered for at least several months.

FINGER-JOINTED LUMBER, below, is designed to receive a painted finish; avoid transparent finishes with this product.

PRESSURE-TREATED LUMBER, opposite, is used for structural purposes and for porch decking.

Finger-Jointed Lumber. If you are sold on the idea of using solid wood for your trim, and are certain that the finish will be either paint or opaque stain, you can consider finger-jointed lumber as a cost-cutting alternative. Some people consider finger-jointed stock to be an engineered wood product, but it really falls in its own category of material. To create finger-jointed stock, short lengths of clear lumber are joined end-to-end with interlocking glue joints, forming a continuous board, often up to 16 feet long. Pine, cedar, and redwood are all commonly sold as finger-jointed stock, and for nonstructural uses, these can provide a considerable savings over solid lumber. Make sure to check that the glue used in the joints is rated for exterior use. Sometimes this type of material comes with a factory-applied primer coat, a great bonus that can save you a lot of time and money.

FINGER JOINT

Finger-jointed stock is clearly not an option for any use that has a structural component. And even though the stock is carefully manufactured to yield a smooth surface, different pieces of wood will expand and contract at different rates, and the joints between the sections can become visible over time; this means that it's extremely important that you seal all stock completely before installation, and maintain the finish in good condition over the years.

Nominal versus Actual Lumber Sizes

NOMINAL SIZE	ACTUAL SIZE
1 x 2	3/4 x 1 1/2
1 x 3	3/4 x 2 1/2
1 x 4	3/4 x 3 1/2
1 x 6	3/4 x 5 1/2
1 x 8	3/4 x 7 1/4
1 x 10	3/4 x 9 1/4
1 x 12	3/4 x 11 1/4
5/4 x 2	1 1/8 x 1 1/2
5/4 x 4	1 1/8 x 3 1/2
5/4 x 6	1 1/8 x 5 1/2
5/4 x 8	1 1/8 x 7 1/4
5/4 x 10	1 1/8 x 9 1/4
5/4 x 12	1 1/8 x 11 1/4

Note: Redwood and cedar 1-by lumber is sometimes sold in finished thickness of 11/16 in. instead of a full 3/4 in., and 5/4 lumber is sometimes sold in finished thickness of 1 in.

Alternatives to Solid Wood

As demand has grown for solid wood trim stock, the quality of available material has declined and the price has risen dramatically. So, it's only natural that, seeing an opportunity, the building products industry has stepped in to provide alternative products. If your trim will get a painted or opaque stain finish, the material options expand to include a wide range of synthetic and engineered-wood products. And while you might think that these are inferior to "real" wood, some can present advantages in appearance and ease of installation. And while some might be cheap alternatives to wood trim, other products cost quite a bit more than even the most desirable wood species, and perform extremely well. Some of these materials are not usually considered for do-it-yourself projects, and you may not find all of them in your local home center. But if you visit an old-fashioned lumberyard, you will generally be able to find, or order, the more obscure materials. In addition, all manufacturers now have Web sites that provide supplier information.

FIBER-CEMENT SIDING AND TRIM PIECES are a popular alternative to solid wood. The material is durable and takes a painted finish.

Hardboard. This trim material is made from chips of hardwood that are heated with steam and hot water and then ground into a fibrous mash that is mixed with resin. Then it is heated and pressed into uniform trim stock in widths from 4 to 12 inches and 16-foot lengths. Some manufacturers add a resin-soaked paper facing to the material to create a super-smooth surface for painting. Working with hardboard can present some challenges because it can be tough to nail and must be completely sealed on all surfaces to prevent swelling or buckling. Most manufacturers recommend that you should drive nails flush to the surface and not countersink the heads—this is important to protect the core stock from moisture infiltration. Any holes must be thoroughly filled and sealed.

Fiber-Cement. Another composite product is fiber-cement trim. As a mixture of wood fiber, Portland cement, and sand, it is durable, extremely stable, fire-resistant, and pretty impervious to weather, insects, and ultraviolet radiation. Trim components are designed to be used as part of a complete siding system, so most of these elements are just $\frac{7}{16}$ inch thick. Different thickness trim boards are available from some manufacturers in a lower-density formulation. Some of these products come with one smooth and one textured side, so you can choose the type of appearance the trim will display.

Working with fiber-cement trim is different from working with wood. It is hard to cut, so carbide blades are necessary, and even they can still dull quickly. Cutting will also generate a lot of nasty dust, so proper dust masks are necessary. And it is tricky to nail, requiring a good nail gun that is properly adjusted for the material. On the plus side, expect a painted finish to last a long time because there is virtually no seasonal expansion nor contraction in the stock.

Laminated Veneer Lumber. Laminated veneer lumber (LVL) is a lot like high-grade plywood. Layers of veneers are glued together under high pressure, with an exterior-grade glue, to form lumber-like trim stock. A resin-soaked paper facing is bonded to the outside face to provide a smooth, defect-free surface. This material has some attractive benefits for trim use. It's available in standard thicknesses for one-by and 5⁄4 stock and can be custom ordered in a variety of sizes from 11⁄16 to 1⅜ inches thick. LVL is easy to cut and install with normal carpentry tools and has no defects to generate waste. It is dimensionally stable and takes a nice finish.

VINYL PRODUCTS, above, are making inroads into the exterior trim area. The railing system and arbor shown are vinyl products.

MANY ALTERNATIVES, such as fiber-cement, **right,** are available in siding and matching or contrasting trim components.

Plastic Materials

Cellular PVC. This is one of the newer, and most promising, products. Trim stock is manufactured in standard sizes and it provides many advantages in application and durability. PVC is extremely weather resistant and is a consistent material and density throughout the stock. It is not affected by rain or snow and will hold a painted finish for a long time. One of its more interesting features is that it's not even necessary to paint the trim, and it will still hold up to the elements. You can use traditional woodworking tools to cut and install PVC trim, and if necessary, it can be glued using the same cement as plumbing pipe. While it doesn't react to water, PVC will expand and contract with changes in temperature—more than a comparable piece of wood. So it's important that joints are designed to hide any gaps that might occur. And as a plastic product, PVC will inevitably get brittle in very cold weather and could crack if nails or screws are placed too close to the edge or end of a piece. PVC trim is definitely considered a high-end product and commands a premium price. Expect to pay at least as much as you would for western red cedar—maybe a bit more.

Polyurethane. Many decorative trim elements, such as medallions, brackets, and the like, are fashioned from polyurethane. The benefit is that polyurethane can be molded into just about any shape, making complex designs that would be difficult to fashion from real wood readily available in a material that looks like wood.

PRODUCTS MADE OF PVC, below left, are weather resistant and long lasting. PVC is available as both boards and panels.

ALTHOUGH IT LOOKS LIKE BEAD BOARD, below right, this entry ceiling is made of cellular PVC material.

Panel Products

If your trim job includes wide soffits or decorative wall panels, you will need some type of panel stock. Of course, it's possible to use solid wood boards to fill in a wide expanse of trim—either square edge or tongue-and-groove material can be used. But for the most economical use of materials and labor, as well as best performance, a manufactured panel is often the best choice. Each proprietary trim product has its own system for soffit construction, but you don't need to swear allegiance to any particular manufacturer. It's fine to mix and match products for reasons of appearance, availability, cost, or performance, so consider the options before making a decision.

Construction Plywood. In addition to the products already discussed, there are other panel products to consider. First among these is traditional exterior-grade plywood. For soffit construction, you can select A/B grade, sanded exterior fir or rough-sawn cedar panels in thicknesses from ¼ to ¾ inch. These and other exterior-grade panels are usually sold in 4 × 8-foot sheets, so they can be cut to any size a job requires. You will also find various grooved and beaded panels designed for porch ceiling applications that can be used for areas like soffits that are protected from direct weather exposure.

Medium Density Overlay. For many years, sign makers have used panel stock that is called Medium Density Overlay or MDO. This material is exterior-grade plywood that has a resin-saturated fiber facing on its surface. The dense core is virtually impervious to water and insect damage and the smooth face provides an excellent paint-grade finish. MDO is available in. ⅜-, ½-, and ¾-inch thicknesses in 4 × 8-foot sheets. You can purchase material with facing on either one or both sides of the panel.

SOLID WOOD BEAD BOARD is the gold standard for porch ceilings, but panel products that look like bead board provide a realistic finish at a fraction of the cost.

SEMITRANSPARENT STAINS, above, allow the natural grain of the wood on this door to be visible. Stains used by themselves offer minimal protection.

CLEAR PRESERVATIVES, such as the type used on the shingles **below,** tend to darken the wood.

FINISHING MATERIALS

ALTHOUGH THERE ARE A FEW TRIM MATERIALS that can be left unfinished—cedar, redwood, and PVC—it's really not recommended as a long-lasting treatment. Both cedar and redwood will weather and turn gray with exposure to ultraviolet light and water, and the weathering process will eventually cause the wood to split and develop a rough surface. While PVC will not break down if left unpainted, it is only available in white and it will look like plastic unless it receives some texture from brush strokes. In most cases, some type of penetrating or surface finish should be applied, and the decision as to what type of finish to use is directly linked to the trim material used on the job. There are a few major classifications of finish types to be considered, and within those groups, you will find a wide variety of manufacturers and specific products from which to choose. In addition, many suppliers provide a range of quality and cost choices for a particular class of finish, so you can usually find a product for any need and budget. But because most people would like to extend the time required between applications, it's generally a good idea to opt for the premium product.

Types of Finishes

If your trim is solid wood, you have the widest variety of finishing choices; clear, semitransparent stain, opaque stain, and paint are all viable options. But there are some choices that are only appropriate for solid wood—clear and semitransparent stains—and both of these are considered penetrating finishes since they soak into the wood and do not form a surface film.

Transparent Water-Repellent Preservatives. This type of preservative can be used for cedar, cypress, or redwood trim when the desire is to maintain the natural color of the wood. These are usually a mixture of preservative, resin, solvent, and a small amount of wax, without any coloring pigments. For best performance, look for a product that offers protection from ultraviolet radiation.

When applied to a wood surface, these materials will darken it like water does and keep it from turning gray when exposed to the weather. Just like any other finish, these preservatives need to be reapplied periodically to maintain their protective function. A water-repellent preservative can also be applied to bare wood before priming and painting, but it is important to check the compatibility of the products to ensure that the paint won't peel. Always carefully read the labels on all products, and follow the manufacturer's instructions. As a pre-painting treatment, a preservative can help prevent water from migrating into the cell structure of the wood, particularly at joints and exposed end grain; this can help extend the life of a paint job by several years.

Penetrating finishes, by their nature, do not protect a wood surface the way a surface coating might. Consequently, these need to be reapplied more frequently than another type of finish. Fortunately, though, because these materials are absorbed into the wood surface, very little preparation is required for re-coating, and the job is relatively simple.

Semitransparent Stains. This type of stain contains a moderate amount of pigment in order to allow the natural grain of the wood to remain visible. Applied by either brush or roller, these stains soak into the wood surface, leaving no surface film. Many of these products also contain some type of wood preservative or water repellent. Semitransparent stains are often used on rough-sawn trim and siding materials, and they are particularly well suited for rustic styles of trim. Most stains are alkyd- or oil-based formulations, but some latex products are also offered. While the latex products are not as readily absorbed into the wood structure as the oil-based stains, they do offer the same advantages as latex paint—ease of application, fast drying, simple cleanup, and low toxicity.

Solid Color (Opaque) Stains. Solid color, or opaque, stains are also offered in both oil-based and latex formulations. Much like thinned paint, these products fall somewhere between a penetrating and surface coating. The oil-based stain is absorbed more readily into the wood surface, while the latex stain tends to sit on the surface. These are mixed with a much higher percentage of pigment than semitransparent stains. As a result, you will find that the natural wood color and grain is obscured by this product, while the general texture of the wood remains visible. For natural wood trim you can use either oil- or latex-based stain, but for composite products like hardboard or fiber-cement, latex is generally recommended. In addition, for some substrates a compatible primer is recommended before applying the stain.

WOOD SHAKES AND SHINGLES benefit from the application of some sort of preservative. The coating protects the wood, and it slows down the weathering of the material.

PAINT

EVERYONE IS FAMILIAR WITH PAINT. As the most popular finish for wood, metal, composite, and plastic items, we know that we can rely on paint to shield and decorate a surface. For exterior trim, paint is one of the most protective finishes, and one of the most versatile. It can be applied to any type of material, the range of colors available is almost infinite, and you can select the degree of sheen, from dead flat to high gloss, to achieve just the look you desire. Because paint is a surface coating, it provides both protection and the ability to hide small defects in a surface. With

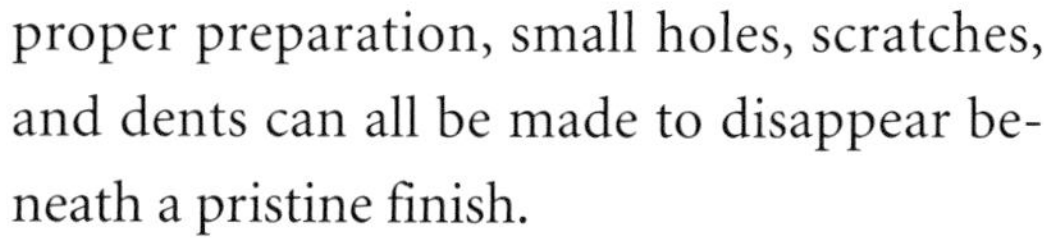

proper preparation, small holes, scratches, and dents can all be made to disappear beneath a pristine finish.

Types of Paint. It used to be the case that alkyd or oil-based paint was considered to be the premium choice for exterior paint. But with recent air quality regulations, alkyd house paint is becoming difficult, if not impossible, to obtain in many locations. And when you can find it, alkyd enamel is often sold in small (quart) containers only, making it an expensive option for a large trim job. Fortunately, paint manufacturers have made great efforts to improve the performance of their latex products, so that now latex is generally accepted as a first-class coating for exterior work. Of course, latex paint offers the substantial advantages of low toxicity, water cleanup, and fast drying times, so it's not too hard to settle on it rapidly becoming the only game in town.

With latex paint, the premium formulations are based on all-acrylic resin. As you might expect, these are more expensive than those based on acrylic mixtures, but the increased adhesion and toughness will give you a much longer lasting paint job.

For a first-quality application, expect that a full primer coat will be necessary. It is especially important that the primer and top coat be fully compatible, and that the manufacturer's directions for application be carefully followed.

COLOR SELECTION, above, plays an important role in the look of a trimwork element.

PORCH PAINTS, left, are formulated to stand up to the abuse these areas receive.

ALL PAINT JOBS, opposite, rely on careful and thorough prep work for success.

Matching the Finish to the Trim Material

TRIM MATERIAL	TYPE OF FINISH			
	Clear/Penetrating	Semitransparent Stain	Solid Color Stain	Paint
Solid Wood	X	X	X	X
Finger-Jointed Wood			X	X
LVL			X	X
Hardboard			X	X
Fiber-Cement			X	X
OSB			X	X
PVC			X	X

CHAPTER 9

MAINTENANCE & REPAIRS

ONCE YOU UNDERSTAND the elements and function of exterior trim, you may be inspired to gain some hands-on experience in repairing parts that have suffered the ravages of extreme weather, insect attack, or just benign neglect. Of course, there are some projects that should only be tackled by a knowledgeable contractor, with all the tools, time, and resources required. But there are plenty of trim repair jobs that any willing homeowner can tackle and execute successfully. If you're a complete novice in the area of home repair, it's best to begin with maintenance rather than demolition. And once you've overcome the initial intimidation of getting your hands dirty, you can undertake some repairs.

For a beginner, the key to success is to limit the scope of your repair job. By following a logical and thorough approach to the task, you can achieve great results and build confidence for more ambitious projects. And if you find that the hands-on approach is not one of your strengths, these descriptions will help you understand the work your contractor does to repair the trim on your home.

DIAGNOSING PROBLEMS

CONSCIENTIOUS HOMEOWNERS will take an active interest in the appearance of their homes. An overall glance at the structure may give a general impression of the state of things, but home maintenance requires a more careful examination of some details to keep small problems from blossoming into major repairs. And when a significant repair is needed, it's best to get it done before it becomes even more serious.

Start your exterior diagnosis by examining the finish on the trim. If the trim has a painted finish, look for excessive chalking, cracks, peeling, and missing chips. Areas that receive the most sun and rain exposure will degrade first. Wood trim that has a clear or semitransparent stain finish will not show peeling but may exhibit other signs of distress. If you notice dark stains coming from nailholes or discolored or cupped trim members, these are signs that moisture has migrated into the wood structure.

Inspect the caulk joints between trim and siding. A proper caulk joint will protect these areas from moisture and insect infiltration

Analyzing Paint Problems

PAINT IS THE FIRST LINE OF PROTECTION for your home. So any condition that causes a paint job to fail should be fixed before the wall is repainted. Below are some of the most common signs of paint failure. They are caused by poor workmanship, the wrong materials, or conditions inside the home.

BLISTERS are caused by applying paint in direct sunlight or moisture migrating from inside the wall. Correct moisture problems before repainting.

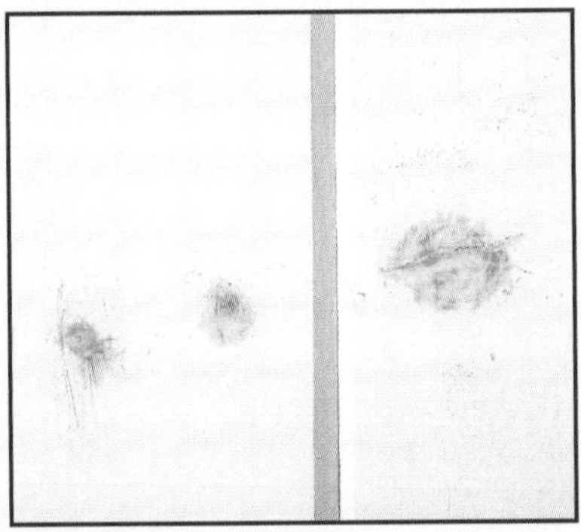

BLEEDING is a sign that uncoated nailheads were used during installation or wood knots were not primed correctly when the wall was painted.

ALLIGATORING occurs when one layer of paint does not adhere to a previous layer. The only solution is to scrape to bare wood, prime, and repaint.

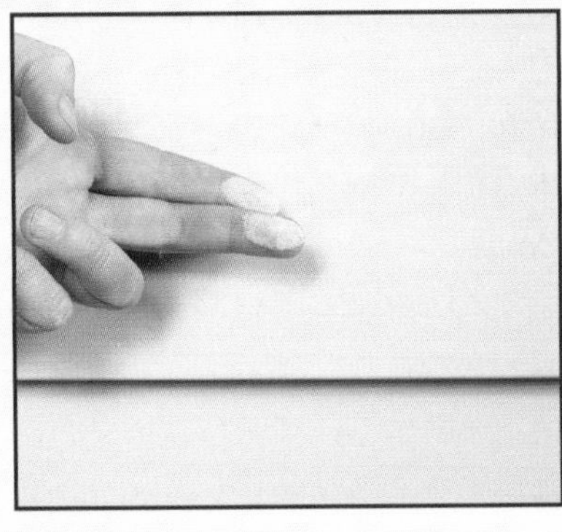

EXCESSIVE CHALKING can prevent a good paint job. All paints break down over time. To repaint, clean thoroughly before painting.

SMART TIP FIXING PAINT PROBLEMS

Although it may seem unlikely, sometimes problems with exterior paint can be traced to a source inside the home. Bubbles in the paint surface can appear, on both siding and trim, as a result of moisture migrating through the wall surface from the inside and becoming trapped beneath an impermeable layer of paint. This condition is often a result of a combination of factors, such as an inadequate vapor barrier on the interior walls, lack of ventilation in the kitchen or bath, and an exterior membrane that does not allow the house to "breathe."

To remedy this problem, consider adding a vent fan over the stove or tub to pull excess moisture from the air before it can enter the exterior wall space.

and will prevent energy-robbing drafts. Caulk that has become hard and dry, either pulling away from the siding or trim material on either side of the joint or missing completely, needs to be replaced.

Check the condition of glazing compound on the exterior of windows. This material, like caulk, can become dry and hard over time. If you notice cracks in the surface or missing sections, these need repair to maintain a good seal.

Aluminum trim is particularly susceptible to wind damage. Look for pieces that are beginning to come loose. In extreme cases, trim material can tear through the nails that hold it to the building; soffits, fascia, and rake trim are areas that often need attention.

Any area where a vertical trim member rests on a horizontal surface is a potential trouble spot because water can pool there and, over time, cause rot or create an environment attractive to insects. If you suspect serious damage, you can use an old screwdriver or awl to poke into the trim material; if the tool pierces the trim easily, the part needs to be repaired or replaced.

CHECK THE JUNCTIONS where siding meets a corner board or some other trim element. This joint is usually caulked, and caulk can wear out after a time.

REMOVE DAMAGED PAINT, above, before repainting. A heat gun aids in paint scraping.

INSPECT PAINT AND FLASHING regularly. Note the condition of the column bases **below.**

MAKING REPAIRS

ONCE YOU'VE DISCOVERED some sections of exterior trim that need attention, the next step is to form a plan to remedy those problems. Sometimes the solution is simple but still requires an investment in "sweat equity" to resolve the trouble. This type of repair is typified by trim with paint that is seriously weathered. If no other problems are apparent, this job involves careful prep work to ensure a smooth surface and a good bond between the new paint and old trim.

Paint Problems. Whenever a piece of trim has loose, blistered, or peeling paint, it is necessary to scrape the surface to remove those defective areas and provide a solid base for the new finish. Use a heavy-duty paint scraper or putty knife to get rid of the most obvious problems; then follow with an abrasive wheel or power sander for the more subtle areas. These techniques generally leave an uneven surface, because some sections remain painted and others bare. In these cases, you can patch the low spots with exterior spackling compound and sand it smooth before applying the primer coat. If the existing paint is in sound condition but is starting to look dull, you can often limit your prep to cleaning the surface before repainting.

Fixing Flashing. Old window and door flashing can become cracked and start to leak. If the crack is small, you can try to seal the defect with silicone or another high-performance sealant. But if the flashing is really degraded, the solution is to carefully pry out the old part and replace it with a new aluminum Z-flashing; the long leg of the flashing must be worked under the siding, and the other leg fits over the window or door head casing.

Sometimes a portion of a trim piece is so rotten that it cannot be patched. One example might be a window sill that has rotted at one end while the rest remains in fine condition. Because replacing the entire sill is difficult and risky, you can cut and chisel out a limited section of the sill and install a patch, also called a "Dutchman."

Window Sill Repair

WINDOWS ARE EXPOSED to harsh weather conditions, and water that is trapped behind casings or sills will cause damage to the part. In these cases, remove the damaged sections and replace with new wood.

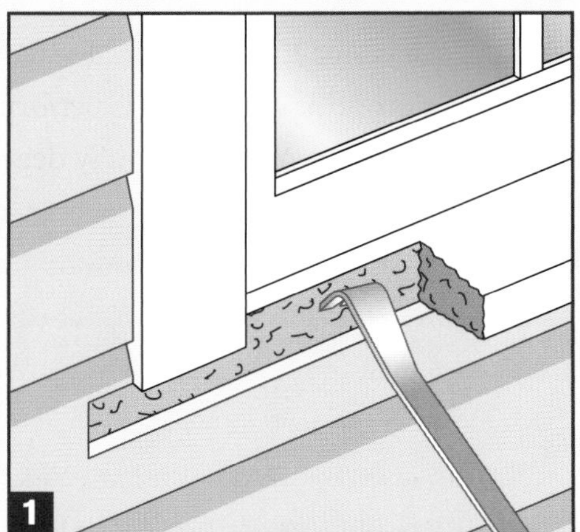

REMOVE THE DAMAGED WOOD. Use a pry bar or an old chisel to remove the loose material. Anything that comes away easily is damaged.

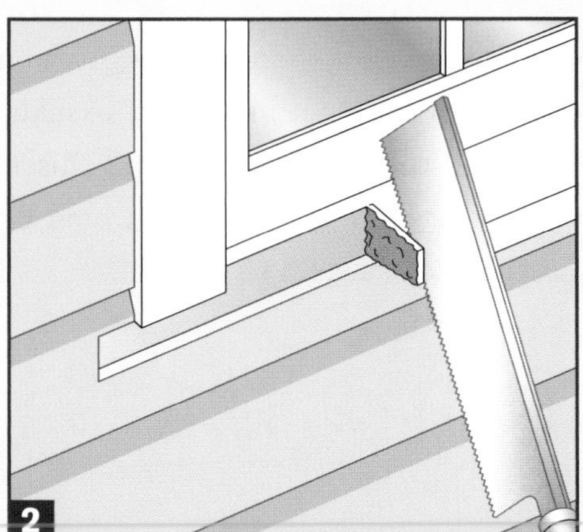

TO CREATE A NEAT JOINT, mark the cut by scoring the cut line with a utility knife. Then use a backsaw or Japanese handsaw to make the cut.

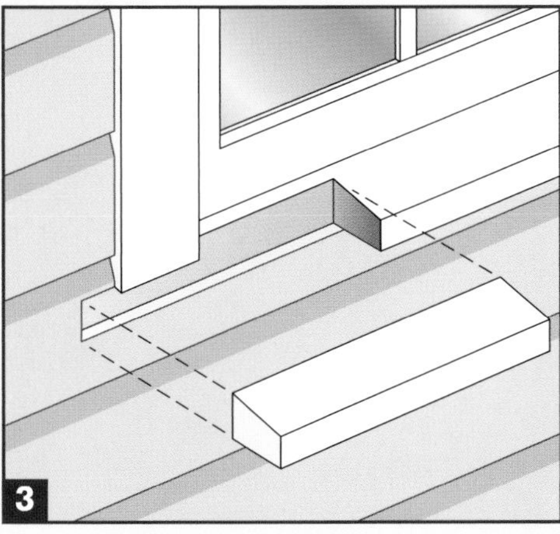

CUT A NEW SECTION to replace the old. Test fit the patch. Then apply a waterproof glue to the window and to the patch. Drive a corrosion-resistant screw through the patch into the window frame.

CHECK WOOD TRIM, above, where it is most vulnerable. Pay careful attention to trim components located at ground level.

WINDOW FLASHING plays an important role in weatherproofing. Inspect head flashing, **below,** and replace any damaged material.

NEGLECT CAN TAKE ITS TOLL. In many cases, repairing and refinishing a component can undue the damage caused by neglect.

SMART TIP INSECT SOLUTION

In some areas, insect damage by carpenter ants, termites, and powderpost beetles is almost epidemic. The combination of intense damp weather and native insect habitats can combine to make this a constant concern for the homeowner. If you find that this is a problem in your home, you can add some ammunition to your struggle by treating new wood trim parts with boron-based insecticide and preservative.

REPLACING DAMAGED TRIMWORK

EVEN IF YOU ARE DILIGENT about maintaining the exterior of your home, problems can develop that mandate replacement of trim parts. Severe weather, insect infestation, failure of paint or caulk can all quickly lead to pockets of rotten wood, and when you finally notice the damage, it's too late for a partial fix. In most cases, it's not too difficult to replace a piece of trim, but it is important to follow the proper procedures to guarantee that the new part lasts and fulfills both the decorative and protective functions it is designed to perform.

The first step in removing the old trim is to cut the caulk joint between the trim and surrounding siding. You can use a utility knife to score the joint, or you can scrape the caulk from the joint with a chisel. Next, carefully slip a flat pry bar under one edge of the trim piece and gently work the trim loose. Depending on the type of trim and its location, you might need to slide a piece of scrap wood under the bar to increase the leverage and protect surrounding siding or window and door jambs. Resist the impulse to get too aggressive in removing the trim because you do not want to damage other parts while trying to repair the piece of your initial focus.

Replacement Parts. For painted wood trim, the best replacement stock is usually pine or cedar as these species are readily available, relatively inexpensive, and accept paint well. But, if the trim is finished with a clear or stained finish, it is important to use the same species as the original trim for the replacement part.

If necessary, patch or replace the building paper behind the trim element; then measure the opening for the replacement part. Cut the piece to size; check that it fits properly; and prime the piece on all sides, letting it dry before installing it. If the trim is a horizontal part, such as a head casing on a door or window, check that the flashing between the siding and trim is intact and replace it if cracked or deformed. Next, fit the piece into position and nail it to the wall with rust resistant nails. Set and fill all nailholes and caulk the joint between the siding and trim.

PORCH ELEMENTS, below, should be inspected regularly for possible damage.

DECORATIVE DESIGNS, right, are available in polyurethane for easy replacement.

RESTORATION OR REPLACEMENT?

IN THE WORLD OF EXTERIOR TRIM, restoration generally refers to an effort to return a damaged part to its original appearance. This approach is most often appropriate for an older home in which the architectural details are unique, of historical significance, or simply are not readily available as replacement parts. If your home is an example of one of the notable periods of our architectural history, such as Victorian, Federal, or Arts and Crafts, there can be an increased motivation for restoration because preserving original details can be essential to maintaining the value of the property. People who are fans of period dwellings are often quite well versed in the particular architectural details of a style, and the consistency of these details is important in preserving the historical legacy of a building.

Of course, your home needn't be 100 years old to qualify for a restoration. Many more recent trim profiles that were once considered standard are no longer readily available. As specialty lumberyards and millwork houses have been replaced by home centers, the selection of stock products has been steadily shrinking. Simplified versions of once-elaborate moldings have become the norm, and replacement parts can be difficult to locate.

So, the restoration of a particular piece of trim can involve a variety of materials and resources. In the most typical case, the focus of the effort is a part that has become too rotten for a simple patch and a replacement part would need to be custom made. Rather than commissioning the custom replacement, a restorer could remove the rotten material, stabilize the margins of the original part with a wood preservative or stabilizer, and then use an epoxy resin or wooden patch to fill the gap. Then, using sanders, rifflers, and rotary shaping tools, the original profile of the trim can be carved to return the trim to its initial form.

THE COMPONENTS ON PERIOD HOUSES, such as this example of Gothic Revival architecture, are often candidates for restoration.

PVC or Real Wood?

PVC TRIM IS A GREAT ALTERNATIVE to solid wood trim. It's manufactured in most of the same nominal sizes as standard pine and cedar trim. And you can find many specialty items, particularly fence components like posts, balusters, and lattice panels. These products are practically impervious to insect and moisture damage and can be painted just like solid wood.

Some 5⁄4 (1¼-inch) stock is available, so high-end trim treatments, like fluted casing boards, can be fabricated with a router and a simple core box bit. In fact, PVC stock can be cut, drilled, and sanded like solid wood. And it's simple to glue together with a special cement, like the adhesive used to join plastic plumbing pipes.

There are only two notable drawbacks to this material. First is the price. It costs almost twice as much as standard No. 2 pine stock and nearly 50 percent more than cedar trim boards. The other shortcoming is that PVC can be brittle in cold weather. So you should probably avoid installing this material in the middle of the winter. And if you are trying for a historically accurate restoration, then this material can't replace real wood. Check with the local historical society for advice.

SOME DETAILS are difficult to find in the normal building-products marketplace. For something that can't be easily purchased, check with specialty lumberyards and woodworking shops for the possibility of custom work.

PORCH RAILINGS & FLOORS

Porches are typically enclosed with a system of rails and decorative spindles, often terminating at columns that support the porch roof. Over time, these details are subject to deterioration due to weathering and insect damage, and severely degraded spindles are prime candidates for restoration.

Spindles come in a wide range of styles, from simple square stock to elaborate turned profiles with ball, cove, bead, and tapered sections. On many old porches, the spindles are unique, and replacement parts are generally not available, unless you can find them at an architectural salvage dealer. So, for spindles with damaged sections, restoration is your best option.

The most likely area of decay in a spindle is the junction of the spindle with the bottom rail. Moisture from rain and snow that accumulates on the horizontal rail can easily migrate into the end grain of a spindle and cause the wood to rot or become attractive to termites or carpenter ants. In many cases, you can repair this type of damage, in place, by patching with a two-part resin filler.

The first thing to do is to remove the damaged section of the spindle. Keep in mind that it's important to be extremely careful when first attacking a damaged area. The goal of a restoration is to preserve as much of the original detail as possible, so use the least aggressive tool that will still do the job. A small, old chisel is a good tool to use to determine the extent of the damage. Once the rotten portion is removed, saturate the margins of the repair area with a wood stabilizer. Follow the directions on the package for application instructions. Next, use the wood filler to patch the area; it's best to slightly overfill the repair to allow for shrinkage and shaping. When the filler is completely dry, duplicate the contours of the original spindle by carving and sanding it with abrasive tools.

TONGUE-AND-GROOVE PORCH BOARDS require special attention when replacing them. **Step 1:** use a circular saw to cut through a damaged board; use an old chisel to remove the waste. **Step 2:** make sure the patch can be attached to the porch framing. **Step 3:** slide the new board into position. Here, the groove of the new board engages the tongue of the adjacent board.

1

2

Repairing Porch Floors. Broken or rotted porch deck boards should be replaced. This is relatively easy for square-edged face-nailed boards, which can simply be pried up with a wrecking bar and a new board nailed in its place.

Replacing tongue-and-groove blind-nailed boards is more work. First, use a circular saw to cut through the middle of one of the damaged boards. Then pry each half out. If you are replacing only part of a board, make a cut above a floor joist. Pull the nails, and remove the fragments of the tongues or grooves. Then fit in new boards, blind-nailing as you go until you reach the last board. Cut the bottom flange off the grooved edge. Slip the tongue into the groove of the adjacent board, and face-nail near the edge with the single-flange groove. If you can slide the new board in from the end, you don't need to remove the flange.

PORCH SPINDLES, above, are subject to damage, especially where the spindle meets the bottom rail. In many cases, you can make repairs without removing the spindle by applying wood-repair products.

COLUMN RESTORATION

COLUMNS AND DECORATIVE PILASTERS really add a sense of style and elegance to a home. Of course, in the case of columns, their decorative function is only part of the story, because they also support a beam or porch roof, while pilasters simply suggest a structural role in the building. But both elements share a particular weakness when used in outdoor locations. Because the bases rest directly on the porch floor, it is inevitable that they will be subjected to snow drifts, ice buildup, and puddles of rain that settle on the deck. And, due to a lack of maintenance, poor original materials, faulty design, or shoddy workmanship, these elements can begin to decay.

Fortunately, most column and pilaster bases are independent elements and can be repaired, or replaced if necessary, without disturbing the rest of the structure. For a plinth base, or column base that requires only cosmetic repair, two-part epoxy filler is an option for replacing rotten wood. Once the decayed material is removed with an old chisel, follow a similar procedure as for a spindle repair—soak the margins of the remaining base with thin epoxy resin, and then fill the hole with thickened epoxy. After letting the material completely dry, shape the patch to match the original base profile.

Column Bases. For column bases that are more seriously deteriorated, the base must be removed to execute a proper repair.

COLUMN BASES are prone to damage. If you are lucky, you may be able to repair the base while salvaging the rest of the column. **Step 1:** the damaged base will be replaced by a molded base and aluminum pedestal. **Step 2:** after installing jacks or posts for support, remove the column. In this case, the damage could be cut away using a saw.

First, provision needs to be made to relieve the weight that the column supports. This is easily done by using a temporary 4×4 post as a brace, or use a jack to provide support. The next step involves removing the nails that hold the base to both the post and porch floor. It's generally possible to work a hacksaw blade between the parts to cut the existing nails; often these nails will be rusted as a result of the wood decay—rust-resistant nails were not often used in old construction.

Once the base is free, it is much easier to evaluate its condition and cut away the damaged portion. Cut a patch from a rot-resistant wood like cedar, redwood, or cypress, and use a waterproof glue to join it to the base. In this instance, it's best to use an epoxy adhesive because it will hold up best in this stressful application.

Once the patch has been shaped to match the original form of the base, treat the entire piece with a wood preservative; then prime it and give it one coat of finish paint before reinstalling it. Slip it into position, and nail it to both the column and porch floor.

Another option is to cut away the base and replace it with a cast-stone molding and aluminum base plate.

WHEN MAKING COLUMN REPAIRS, you will need to support the structure. Install 4x4 posts or floor jacks under the beam. Toenail posts to the porch floor.

PAINTING

THE CONCEPT OF RESTORATION need not be limited to the repair of rotten or damaged portions of house trim. In fact, the most frequent restoration projects have to do with more superficial details—and that means paint. For a successful paint job, it is critical that you, or your painting contractor, take the time and effort to properly prepare all surfaces. This prep work will normally include washing all trim and siding, scraping areas that have peeling or blistered paint, spackling to fill holes or low spots in the old finish, sanding to level the filler, and either spot priming patched areas or applying a full primer coat to the entire house.

Of course, preparing a house for repainting involves a great amount of work. But, for many people, the most difficult part of the job is deciding on the colors that will be used for the finish coat. For those homes that fall into a distinct architectural style, there is considerable precedent and tradition that can guide the color choice. Local museums and historical societies are great sources of information on the appearance of old buildings in a particular location. They can provide photographic and written evidence to document how buildings appeared when new. In addition, most manufacturers of exterior house paint offer collections of complementary colors that are grouped by period and style. Using these tools, you can select one of their color palettes or use them as a starting point for building your own.

When restoring an older home, remember that you are not bound to re-create the original color scheme. But, for those who love historic dwellings, it's usually most satisfying to keep the colors within the traditional range of colors that complement the style of the home.

EVEN IF YOUR HOME ISN'T AN ANTIQUE, it will benefit from a careful selection of the color palette. Many paint manufacturers offer color collections of historical colors that look great on any house.

SMART TIP HISTORIC COLOR CHOICES

In some areas of the country, there are local regulations that cover modifications, or any changes, to historic buildings that have been classified under a "preservation" statute—and that can even include the colors of exterior paint. If you find that your home falls under this type of jurisdiction, the local preservation board will be an excellent source of information regarding appropriate color choices.

PAINT PREP is important to obtain good results, **left.** Prep usually includes washing, scraping, and repairing before priming.

TO BE HISTORICALLY ACCURATE, check with a preservation board to see which colors suit your home before applying a distinctive color scheme, **above.**

ROUTINE MAINTENANCE

THE OLDER THE HOUSE, the more regular the routine maintenance inspections should be.

REPAIR OR REPLACEMENT OF TRIM PARTS can be a pretty substantial job, entailing significant cost, some inconvenience, and a good amount of time devoted to the project—whether you do the work yourself or hire a contractor. In some instances, the factors that contribute to the degradation of a piece of trim are built into the house. For example, the materials used could be of inferior quality or inappropriate for the part, or flashing might be inadequate or badly designed, leading to water infiltration. And sometimes the cause of a problem can be poor execution on the part of the original builder. In any of these cases, it's likely that the problem would arise sooner or later. However, there are plenty of situations where a homeowner's neglect is the cause of a rotten or damaged piece of trim, and these can be avoided with regular examination and maintenance.

Make it a habit to inspect the exterior of your home after every severe weather event. Look for loose or damaged roof shingles, cracked or missing window glazing, and poor caulk joints. Take the time to watch how water drains from the roof and over windows and doors during a rainstorm, to make sure that it is directed away from the trim. Keep trees and bushes trimmed so that they do not

SMART TIP HIDDEN PROBLEMS

While vinyl and aluminum siding and trim are sold as maintenance-free materials, it may be an overly optimistic description of these products. It is true that repainting is not part of the maintenance routine, but there are still some details that need attention to avoid more serious problems.

Since both vinyl and aluminum trim elements cover a wooden substrate, they tend to hide evidence of moisture-related problems. If a leak occurs in the siding or trim, it can remain hidden for a long time. Look for streaks or stains that appear on the siding, trim, or even on the foundation wall. And, since rot can cause nails to become ineffective, loose siding may be a sign of a potential problem.

brush against the house; insects can use this type of growth as a bridge to the building. Notice areas of the trim that show problems in the painted surface—cracks, blisters, or alligator patterns in the paint. Trim with a clear finish might start to show dark stains that extend from nailholes, a sign that moisture is penetrating into the wood.

The routine tasks of washing, caulking, reglazing, sealing, and touching up the paint, while time consuming, can prevent the larger investment necessary for repair.

Of course, some types of maintenance cannot be undertaken in cold or wet weather, so these tasks must wait for the proper season. But, if you make note of those areas that need attention, you can take the first opportunity to do the job and keep the elements at bay.

STONE is not impervious to damage, **left.** Check column bases and the juncture where trimwork meets masonry.

WATER is the enemy. Routinely inspect areas that are out in the weather, **above,** for possible damage.

RESOURCE GUIDE

The following list of manufacturers and associations is meant to be a general guide to additional industry and product-related sources. It is not intended as a listing of products and manufacturers represented by the photographs in this book.

BOOKS

A Field Guide to American Houses
Virginia & Lee McAlester
Alfred A. Knopf,
Knopf Publishing Group, 1984

American Homes: An Illustrated Encyclopedia of Domestic Architecture
Lester Walker
Black Dog & Leventhal Publishers, Inc., 2002

American Houses: A Field Guide to the Architecture of the Home
Gerald Foster
Houghton Mifflin Co., 2004

American House Styles: A Concise Guide
John Milnes Baker
W. W. Norton & Company, Inc., 2002

House Styles in America: The Old House Journal Guide to the Architecture of American Homes
James C. Massey and Shirley Maxwell
Viking Penguin, 1995

The Visual Dictionary of American Domestic Architecture
Rachel Carley
Henry Holt & Company, Inc.,1997

PERIODICALS

Old House Journal
1000 Potomac St. NW, Ste. 102
Washington, DC 20007
202-339-0744, ext. 101
www.oldhousejournal.com
Excellent source of information on restoring old houses.

This Old House
1185 Avenue of the Americas, 27th Fl.
New York, NY 10036
212-522-9465
www.thisoldhouse.com
A spin-off of the popular TV show and a source of high-end remodeling practices. Frequently covers restoration work.

The Family Handyman
800-285-4961
www.familyhandyman.com
Good source of do-it-yourself home improvement information.

Preservation Magazine
National Trust For Historic Preservation
785 Massachusetts Ave. NW
Washington, DC 20036-2117
800-944-6847
www.nationaltrust.org
The magazine of the National Trust, chartered by Congress to encourage preservation of both private and public buildings and sites.

Fine Homebuilding
The Taunton Press Customer Support Center
63 South Main St.
Newtown, CT 06470-55068
800-477-8727
www.finehomebuilding.com
Good source of information on high-quality home building practices.

PAINTS

Behr Paints
3400 W. Segerstrom Ave.
Santa Ana, CA 92704
877-237-6158
www.behr.com

Benjamin Moore & Co.
51 Chestnut Ridge Rd.
Montvale, NJ 07645
201-573-9600
www.benjaminmoore.com

California Paints
Corporate Headquarters & Manufacturing
150 Dascomb Rd.
Andover, MA 01810
800-225-1141
www.californiapaints.com

STAINS & PRESERVATIVES

Cabot Stains
800-US-STAIN (800-877-8246)
www.cabotstain.com

Flood Exterior Finishes and Preservatives
The Flood Company
P.O. Box 2535
Hudson, OH 44236-0035
800-321-3444
www.flood.com

Olympic Stains
800-441-9695
www.ppg.com

Glidden Paints
ICI paint Headquarters W
16651 Sprague Rd.
Strongsville, OH 44156
800-GLIDDEN (800-454-3336)
www.glidden.com

Pratt & Lambert Paints
101 Prospect Ave. NW
Cleveland, OH 44115
U.S. 1-800-BUY-PRATT (800-289-7728)
Canada 1-877-772-8898
www.prattandlambert.com

The Sherwin-Williams Company
www.sherwin-williams.com

Sikkens Stains
866-SIKKENS (886-745-5367)
www.nam.sikkens.com

TRIM LUMBER

A & M Wood Specialty
357 Eagle St. N
P.O. Box 32040
Cambridge, Ontario N3H 5M2
Canada
800-265-2759
www.forloversofwood.com

California Redwood Association
888-CALRED-WOOD
www.calredwood.org

Engineered Wood Products Association
6300 Enterprise Ln.
Madison, WI 53719
www.ewpa.com

Southern Pine Council
2900 Indiana Ave.
Kenner, LA 70065
504-443-4464
www.southernpine.com

Western Red Cedar Lumber Association
1501-700 West Pender St.
Vancouver, B.C. V6C 1G8
Canada
866-778-9096
www.wrcla.org

MANUFACTURED PANELS

Canadian Plywood
735 W 15th St.
North Vancouver, B.C. V7M 1T2
Canada
604-981-4190
www.canply.org

Georgia-Pacific
133 Peachtree St. NE
Atlanta, GA 30303
404-652-4000
www.gp.com

Weyerhaeuser
P.O. Box 9777
Federal Way, WA 98063-9777
800-525-5440
www.weyerhaeuser.com

SIDING

Cemplank
26300 La Alameda, Ste. 250
Mission Viejo, CA 92691
877-CEMPLANK (877-236-75265)
www.cemplank.com

CertainTeed
P.O. Box 860
750 E Swedesford Rd.
Valley Forge, PA 19482
800-782-8777
www.weatherboards.com

Pacific Wood Laminates
885 Railroad Ave.
P.O. Box 820
Brookings, OR 97415
541- 469-4177
www.socomi.com
www.pacificwoodlaminates.com

PVC TRIM BOARDS

AZEK Trimboards
801 Corey St.
Moosic, PA 18507
877-ASK-AZEK (877-275-2935)
www.azek.com

Fypon
960 W Barre Rd.
Archbold, OH 43502
800-446-3040
www.fypon.com

James Hardie
26300 La Alameda, Ste. 250
Mission Viejo, CA 92691
888-J-HARDIE (888-542-7343)
www.jameshardie.com

Louisianna-Pacific
LP Marketing Center
P.O. Box 7429
Endicott, NY 13761-7429
888-820-0325
www.lpcorp.com

MANUFACTURED TRIM PRODUCTS

Alexandria Moulding
300 Lasley Ave.
Wilkes-Barre, PA 18706
800-841-8746
www.alexandriamoulding.com

Cemplank
26300 La Alameda, Ste. 250
Mission Viejo, CA 92691
877-CEMPLANK (877-236-7526)
www.cemplank.com

Georgia-Pacific
55 Park Pl.
Atlanta, GA 30303
800-Build-GP (800-284-5347)
www.gp.com

James Hardie
26300 La Alameda, Ste. 250
Mission Viejo, CA 92691
888 J-HARDIE (888-542-7343)
www.jameshardie.com

Temple-Inland
P.O. Drawer N
Diboll, TX 75941
800-231-6060
www.temple.com

CertainTeed
P.O. Box 860
750 E Swedesford Rd.
Valley Forge, PA 19482
800-782-8777
www.weatherboards.com

CMI MiraTec Composite Trim
500 W Monroe St., Ste. 2010
Chicago, IL 60661
800-405-2233
www.craftmasterdoordesigns.com

Fypon
960 W Barre Rd.
Archbold, OH 43502
800-446-3040
www.fypon.com

TrimCraft Inc.
1335-1365 Neptune Dr.
Boynton Beach, FL 33426
561-736-3667
www.trimcraft.net

RESTORATION PRODUCTS

Traditional Building Products
69A Seventh Ave.
Brooklyn, NY 11217
718-636-0788
www.traditionalbuilding.com

GLOSSARY

Back cut The technique of removing stock along the rear surface of a piece of molding to reduce the contact area of the joint. Back cuts are recommended in coped joints to allow maximum flexibility in fitting difficult joints.

Backsaw A hand saw with a rectangular blade that is stiffened by a reinforcing metal spine along the top edge of the blade. Available in a variety of sizes, these saws are used to cut precision joints and are the saw of choice for hand miter boxes.

Baluster A spindle or post that supports a handrail on a stairway or balcony.

Bargeboard A trim board that is attached to the end of a gable roof—also called a vergeboard. Bargeboards are often sawn or carved in ornate patterns.

Bevel An angled cut, other than 90 degrees, into the thickness of a piece of stock.

Cantilever A beam or portion of a building that projects beyond a bearing wall or post and has no visible means of support.

Casing A flat or profiled piece of trim that is used to surround a door or window opening.

Caulk A flexible material that is used to fill gaps and seams between adjacent materials. Caulk is supplied in tubes that require an inexpensive gun applicator to transfer it to the target area. Also called caulking.

Chalk line A string covered with powdered chalk used to mark a straight line between distant points. A chalk-line box opens to accept the powdered chalk, and has a reel inside that allows you to automatically spread chalk on the line as it extends from the box.

Chamfer A shallow, angled cut along the edge or end of a board that is used as a decorative detail.

Clapboards Overlapping horizontal boards used as siding. In most cases, these boards have a tapered or wedge-shaped profile and are installed with the thinner edge at the top.

Coped joint A wood joint in which the end of one piece is cut to match the face profile of the adjacent stock.

Coping saw A handsaw with a thin blade held taut between the ends of a C-shaped frame. The saw is used to make the intricate cuts required for inside corner joints on molding stock.

Corner board A vertical trim member that caps the corner of a building. Siding can be cut square to fit against the corner board and then caulked to provide a watertight joint.

Cornice A molding or assembly of moldings at the junction of a wall and ceiling or a wall and a soffit. Cornice molding can also be applied at the top of a column or pilaster.

Cove A concave profile on a molding.

Crosscut To cut a board perpendicular to the direction of the wood grain.

Crown molding A molding designed to sit at an angle between a wall and ceiling. Crown moldings can also be used as capitals on square columns or between an exterior wall and soffit.

Cupola A small, dome-shaped, ornamental structure that projects above a larger roof. A cupola can be used to provide ventilation or to allow light to enter the building.

Dentil A molding detail that includes alternating blocks and spaces—suggestive of a row of teeth.

Dormer A vertical window that interrupts the surface of a sloping roof.

Eave The edge of a roof that extends beyond the exterior wall of a building.

Entablature A molded, decorative horizontal band that forms the crowning feature at the top of a building wall or other architectural element, located above a column, pilaster, or casing.

Fascia A flat, exterior, horizontal trim board that caps the rafter tails at the edge of a roof.

Fenestration The arrangement of the window openings in a building.

Finger-joint A means of joining short lengths of lumber together to form a long board or piece of molding stock. Interlocking "fingers" are cut in the matching ends and the parts are glued together. Finger-jointed stock is suitable only for paint-grade applications.

Flashing A piece of metal or plastic that is installed to prevent water from penetrating a structure. Flashing is commonly used at all exterior building openings, roof intersections, around chimneys, and vent pipes.

Flat-sawn A description of lumber that is cut parallel to one side of a log. Flat-sawn stock often displays cathedral-shaped grain patterns.

Frame construction A system of building construction that relies on regularly spaced vertical and horizontal members to provide the wall, floor, and ceiling structure. The vertical members that make up walls are called studs, and the horizontal members are called joists.

Frieze In exterior trim, a frieze is a horizontal band applied to the wall that lies directly beneath the soffit or eaves.

Gable The triangular portion of a wall that lies between the enclosing lines of a sloping roof.

Gambrel roof A ridged, two-sided roof with two slopes on either side. The lower slope has a much steeper pitch than the upper portion of the roof.

Hardwood Wood that comes from a deciduous tree—one that loses its leaves in winter.

Header A horizontal, weight-bearing support over a room opening such as a door, window, or archway.

Hip roof A roof that slopes from all four sides of a building. The line where two adjacent sloping sides intersect is called the hip and is determined by a hip rafter.

Jambs The top and two sides of a door or window frame that contact the door or sash.

Joist One of a series of regularly spaced, parallel, horizontal members that supports a floor or ceiling.

Kerf The width of a saw-blade cut.

Knot The portion of a branch of a tree that is visible in a piece of lumber. Knots usually appear as dark circles and are commonly considered to be defects.

Level A term used to describe a perfectly horizontal surface. Also a tool used to determine whether a surface is perfectly horizontal.

Lintel A beam, or other horizontal structural member, over an opening such as a window or door. A lintel is designed to carry the weight of material above it.

Millwork A descriptive term used to describe various manufactured wooden trim components such as lumber, moldings, doors, railings, columns, and architectural ornaments.

Miter An angled cut into the face of a piece of stock for a woodworking joint. Typically, the angle of a miter cut is equal to one-half of the total angle of the joint.

Miter saw A saw used to make angled cuts for woodworking joints. Hand-operated and power models are available, as well as models with sliding heads for wide, compound angle cuts.

Molding Decorative strips of wood, composite, or synthetic materials that are used in various trim applications.

Nail set A pointed metal tool used to drive the heads of finishing nails below the wood surface. Sets are available in various sizes to match nail head diameter.

Palladian window A large window divided into three sections. The center section is usually arched and larger than the two flanking side sections—named after the Renaissance architect Andrea Palladio.

Pediment The triangular face of a roof gable. A low-pitched, triangular structure, often found above an entry, or windows, in the Greek Revival style of architecture. A pediment is often accompanied by columns or pilasters.

Pergola A garden structure consisting of an open grid of wood beams supported by posts—often intended to hold climbing plants.

Pilaster A vertical application that projects from a wall surface to suggest the structure of a column. In most cases, base and capital moldings are part of the installation.

Pitch A description of the slope of a roof described in a ratio: inches of rise /12 inches of horizontal run. For example, a 4/12 roof pitch is one that rises 4 inches per foot.

Plinth A block that functions as the base for a traditional door casing or pilaster.

Plumb A term used to describe a perfectly vertical surface.

Porte Cochere A covered, open-sided entry structure, usually over a driveway, that is connected to a house—also called a carport.

Portico A formal entry porch, covered by a roof and supported by columns or posts.

Post and beam A style of construction that relies on heavy timbers, spaced relatively far apart, to provide the framework for a building. The vertical members are called posts and the horizontal members are beams.

Purlin A horizontal roof beam that supports the rafters.

Quarter-sawn A description of lumber that is cut parallel to the radius of the log. Quarter-sawn stock displays grain lines that are parallel with the long edge of the board. Quarter-sawn lumber is also called edge-grain.

Rabbet An open groove cut along the edge or end of a piece of wood. Rabbets are often used to join two pieces of stock at a right angle.

Rafter The parallel structural members of a roof that directly support the roof sheathing.

Rake board A trim board that follows the slope of the roof at its outer edge—generally at a gable end.

Rasp A metal tool with a rough, toothed surface used for rapid removal of wood. Rasps are available in flat and shaped models, as well as various size tooth configurations.

Rip To cut a board parallel to the direction of the wood grain.

Router A power tool that consists of a motor with tool-holding collet held in a portable base. Various cutting tools can be mounted to the end of the rotating shaft for grooving and shaping wood.

Sash The framework of a window in which the panes of glass are mounted.

Scarf joint A joint that is used to join two boards or moldings end to end. Overlapping angled cuts are made in the two parts so that, when assembled, the joint appears invisible.

Scribe To mark and shape a trim member to fit against another irregular surface.

Shim A strip of wood that is used to fill a gap behind a structural or trim item. Most often, narrow tapered shingles are used for this purpose.

Spring angle A pair of angles that explains the way that a crown molding intersects the planes of ceiling and wall. The first number corresponds to the angle between ceiling and the back of the molding and the second is the angle between the wall and back of the molding.

Soffit The finished underside of the roof overhang that fills the space between the exterior wall and fascia.

Softwood Lumber from a coniferous tree. Common species are pine, hemlock, spruce, cedar, and fir.

Square A primary concept in carpentry—that two surfaces are perpendicular, or at 90 degrees to one another. Also, the steel tool used to test that two surfaces are perpendicular.

Stop A strip of wood that abuts a door or window to keep it aligned and operating properly. Stops can have square or shaped edges.

Stud Vertical structural members in house framing, typically of 2×4 or 2×6 lumber.

Toe-nail To drive a nail at an angle, through one framing member and into another, to lock the parts together.

Transom A horizontal divider that separates a large window or door from a smaller window directly above it.

Warp A term indicating that a board is not flat.

INDEX

A

Abrasives, 157
Alkyd house paint, 172
Alligatoring, 176
Aluminum siding, 142–143
  maintenance and, 190
  safety and, 143
Aluminum trim, wind damage to, 177
Arbors, 68, 128–129
  choosing vines for, 129
  flower-covered, 128
  privacy screens for, 128
Arts and Crafts style, 28–29, 182
  characteristics of, 28–29
  dormers in, 28–29
  eave overhangs in, 41
  porches in, 29
  roofs in, 28–29
  windows in, 29
Attic spaces, 33, 42

B

Back priming, 43
Balusters, 96
  design of, 97, 98
Balustrades, 96, 98, 109
Bargeboards
  for gable overhands, 38
  for garages, 117
  geometric patterns in, 38, 39
  problems with, 38
  repairing, 39
Barns, 122–123
  construction of, 122
  maintenance of, 122
  painting, 123
Bay windows in Colonial Revival style, 27
Beaded boards, painting, 101
Belt sanders, 156
Bench-top table saws, 160
Beveled siding, 132
Bleeding, 176
Blisters, 176
Block planes, 154–155
Brackets, 88
Victorian-style, 89
Brick, 138, 148–149
  maintenance of, 148
Brown coat, 146
Bungalow style, 28, 29

C

Canine condos, 121
Cantilevered roof sheathing, 36–37
Capitals, column, 89, 94–95
Casings
  door, 50–57
    painting, 51
  pediments and head, 58–59
  window, 74–77
Caulking, excessive, 176
Caulk joints, inspecting, 176–177
Ceilings, porch, 100–101
  materials for, 100–101
Cellular PVC, 168
Chimneys, Georgian, 14
Circular saws, 158
Colonial Revival style, 26–27
  combining styles, 27
  entries in, 27
  head casings in, 59
  sidelights in, 27
  windows in, 27
Color schemes, 138–139
  complementary, 35
  historic, 189
  in Queen Anne style, 22
  in Victorian styles, 138
Columns, 92–95
  bases of, 186–187
    decay of, 65, 92
    masonry, 29
  capitals for, 89, 94–95
  caring for, 92
  construction of, 93
  Corinthian-style, 89, 95
  Doric-style, 95
  fluted, 98
  for front doors, 54
  Greek Revival, 18
  materials for, 92
  for porte cocheres, 70
  for porticoes, 64
  removing paint from, 98
  restoration of, 186–187
Combination square, 153
Complementary colors, 35
Concrete siding, 142
Condos, canine, 121
Conservatories, 127
Construction plywood, 169
Coping saws, 154
Cordless drill/driver, 155
Corinthian-style columns, 89, 95
Corner boards, 80–81
  caulking, 80–81
  checking junctions and, 177
  lack of, in Shingle style, 24–25
  plywood siding and, 137
  water tables and, 86
Corner windows, 30
Cove molding
  for friezes, 83
  for rake trim, 34
Craftsmen style, 28
  columns in, 92
  pergolas in, 68
Crown molding
  for friezes, 83
  for rake trim, 34
Cupolas, 44–45
  instant, 45
  Italianate style, 21
  mounting, 45
  trim for, 44
  windows in, 21

D

Deadbolts, 51
  keyed cylinders for, 60
Dentils, 34

cleaning, 82
Doorknockers, 54
Doors. *See also* Front doors
double, 21
outer, 66, 67
screen, 56–57
Doric-style columns, 95
Dormers, 42
Arts and Crafts, 28–29
back priming for, 43
Colonial Revival, 27
Greek Revival, 18
shed, 127
trim for, 42
Double doors, 21
Dremel, 161
Drip caps, 77
water tables and, 87
Drip-edge flashing, 34
Dutch door, 71
Dutchman, 178

E

Eaves, 35, 41
Enclosed porches, 110–111
heating, 110, 111
types of, 111
Entries, 49–71
adding glass, 60–63
Colonial Revival, 27
doors and casings, 50–57
Greek Revival, 18
pediments and head casings, 58–59
pergolas, 68–69
porte cocheres, 70–71
porticoes, 64–67
Entry-wall construction, 54
Entryway trim, Federal, 17
Excessive caulking, 176

F

Fanlight windows, 16, 17, 63
Fascia and soffit trimwork, 40–41
ornate, 40
Federal style, 16–17, 182
entryway trim in, 17
friezes on, 84
head casings in, 59
keystone in, 16–17
pilasters in, 88
roofs in, 16–17
windows in, 16
casings of, 74
Fiber-cement siding, 144
Fiber-cement trim, 166–167
Files, 155
Finger-jointed lumber, 164
Finish coat, 146
Finishing materials, 170–171
matching, to trim material, 173
types of finishes, 170–171
Flashing
fixing, 178
inspecting, 178, 179
Floor framing, 112
rot-resistant framing, 112
Floors, porch, 102–104
pressure-treated lumber for, 102
repairing, 184–185
tile for, 102
tongue-and-groove fir boards for, 102–103
Fluted columns, 98
Framing squares, 152
Friezes, 82–85
built-up, 83
decorative, 84–85
detail, 83
Federal style, 84
Georgian-style, 84
Victorian style, 84, 85
Front doors, 71
accessories for, 54
adding glass, 50, 60
casings and, 50–57
double, 21, 54
materials for, 52–53
need for outer, 66, 67
screen, 56–57
shape of curved top, 50
sidelights for, 60
Furnace, heating capacity of, 110

G

Gable overhangs, 36–39
cantilevered roof sheathing for, 36–37
Queen Anne style, 22, 23
trim for, 37
vents for, 46
wasp nesting sites under, 36
width of, 36, 37
Garages
bargeboard for, 117
detached, 116–117
door openers for, 117
Gothic Revival, 116
hardware for, 116
painting, 117
Gazebos, 124–125
screened-in, 124
trimwork on, 124
Georgian style, 13, 14–15, 17
chimneys in, 14
eaves in, 14
enties in, 14
friezes in, 84
pilasters in, 14, 88
porches in, 14
window casings in, 74
windows in, 14
Gingerbread trim, 38, 39
Glass
in front doors, 50, 60
Modern style, 30
in windows, 16
Glazing compound, checking condition of, 177
Glazing point tool, 161
Gothic Revival
bargeboards in, 38
garages in, 116
Graves, Michael, 30
Greek Revival, 17, 18–19, 22
columns in, 18, 92
dormers in, 18
entrance styles in, 18, 19
front doors in, 19
pilasters in, 88
roofs in, 19
windows in, 18–19
Greenhouses, 126–127
add-on, 126
construction of, 126–127
heating, 126
stand-alone, 126

H

Hand saws, 154
Hardboard siding, 145
Hardboard trim, 166
Hardware
deadbolts, 51, 60
for front doors, 54
garages, 116

- locksets, 51
- railing attachment, 96
- shutter, 78

Heat guns, 156
Heating
- of enclosed porches, 110, 111
- of greenhouses, 126

Historical legacy, preserving, 182
House siding, 131–149
- aluminum, 142–143, 190
- brick, 148–149
- concrete, 142
- fiber-cement, 144
- hardboard, 145
- non-wood, 140–144
- plywood, 136–139
- shingles and shakes, 134–135
- stucco, 146–147
- vinyl, 140–141, 190
- wood clapboard, 132–133

House styles, 13–31
- Arts and Crafts, 28–29, 41
- bungalow, 28, 29
- Colonial Revival, 26–27, 59
- Craftsmen, 28, 68, 92
- Federal, 16–17, 59, 74, 88
- Greek Revival, 18, 19
- International, 30
- Italianate, 20–21, 41
- Modern, 13, 30–31
- Prairie, 13, 28, 29
- Queen Anne, 20, 22–23
- Renaissance Revival, 20
- Romanesque Revival, 20
- Second Empire, 20
- Shingle, 24–25
- Villa, 20

I

Insect damage, 180
Instant cupolas, 45
International Style, 30
Italianate style, 20–21
- cupolas in, 21
- eave overhangs in, 41
- porches in, 21
- windows in, 21

J

Jambs, 54
J-channel molding, 142, 143
Jefferson, Thomas, 27
Jig saws, 158–159

K

Keyhole saw, 161
Keystone windows, Federal-style, 16–17

L

Laminated veneer lumber, 167
Landscape, 138
Lap siding, 132
Latex paint, 172
Levels, 153
Library, use of conservatory as, 127
Locksets, replacing, 51
Lookouts, 37
Louvered panels, 67
Louvered shutters, 67
Lumber
- finger-jointed, 164
- laminated veneer, 167
- nominal versus actual sizes, 164
- pressure-treated, 102, 112, 164

M

Mail slots, 54
Maintenance and repairs, 175–191
- column restoration in, 186–187
- deciding between restoration and replacement, 182
- diagnosing problems in, 176–177
- making repairs in, 178–179
- painting in, 188–189
- for porch railings and floors, 184–185
- PVC versus real wood in, 183
- replacing damaged trimwork, 180–181
- routing, 190–191

Mansard roofs, 20
Masonry corners, 81
Medallions, 89
Medium density overlay, 169
Meier, Richard, 30
Metal shears, 161
Miter saws, 159
Modern style, 13, 30–31
- front doors in, 54
- glass in, 30
- windows in, 30

Moisture-related problems, 190
Monticello, 27

N

Non-wood siding, 140–145
- aluminum, 142–143, 190
- concrete, 142
- fiber-cement, 144
- vinyl, 140–141, 190

O

Old chisel, 161
Opaque stains, 171
Outbuildings, 115–129
- arbors, 128–129
- barns, 122–123
- decorative, 120
- garages, 116–117
- gazeboes, 124–125
- greenhouses, 126–127
- storage sheds, 118–121
- Victorian, 121

Outer doors, 66, 67

P

Paint, 172–173
- alkyd, 172
- latex, 172
- removal of, 98, 156

Painting, 188–189
- back priming in, 43
- beaded boards, 101
- door casings, 51
- of garages, 117
- historic color choices in, 189
- spray, 123

Paint problems
- alligatoring, 176
- analyzing, 176
- bleeding, 176
- blisters, 176
- excessive caulking, 176
- fixing, 177, 178

Palladian windows, 27, 63
Panel products, 169
Pediments and head casings, 58–59
- Colonial Revival, 59
- construction of, 58
- Federal style, 59

Pergolas, 68–69, 128

building, 69
gable-style, 68
no-maintenance, 69
peaked, 68
vines for, 68, 69
Pier screens, 106–107
building, 107
materials for, 106
Pilasters, 88–89
brackets for, 89
Georgian style, 14
medallions, 89
Planes, block, 154–155
Plastic material, 168
Playhouses, 120, 121
Plywood, construction, 169
Plywood siding, 136–139
corner boards and, 137
Polyurethane, 168
Porches, 91–113
Arts and Crafts, 29
beaded boards for, 101
ceilings for, 100–101
columns on, 92–95
decorative trimwork for, 104
enclosed, 110–111
heating for, 110
entry, 21
floors for, 102–104
framing, 112
repairing, 184–185
Georgian, 14
glassed-in, 111
Italianate style, 21
ornamental embellishments for, 104
pier screens for, 106–107
railings for, 96–99
repairing, 184–185
raised, 106
roof construction for, 100
screened-in, 57, 111
shingle style, 24
steps for, 108–109
Porte cocheres, 70–71
columns for, 70
need for, 70
Porticoes, 64–67
Post-and-beam construction, 18
Power cutting tools, 158–161
Prairie style, 13, 28, 29
Preservatives, transparent-water-repellent, 170–171
Pressure-treated lumber, 112, 164
exposure to, 112
for porch floors, 102, 112
Privacy screens, 128
Profile gauge, 161
PVC lattice, 106
PVC trim versus wood trim, 183

Q

Queen Anne style, 20, 22–23
color dominance in, 22
distinctive elements in, 22
gables in, 22, 23
spindles in, 22
towers in, 22, 25
windows in, 22

R

Rafters, 40
Railings
attachment for, 96
color of, 97
design of, 98
materials for, 99
porch, 96–99
repairing, 184–185
styles of, 96
types of, 99
Rake board, 34
Rake edge, 34
Rake trim, 34–35
cove molding for, 34
crown molding for, 34
dealing with eaves, 35
installing, 34–35
Random orbital sanders, 156
Rasps, 155
Renaissance Revival style, 20
Repairs. *See* Maintenance and repairs
Restoration tools, 161
Rifflers, 161
Romanesque Revival style, 20
Roofs, 33–47
Arts and Crafts style, 28–29
construction of porch, 100
cupolas, 44–45
dormers, 42–43
fascia and soffit trimwork, 40–41
Federal, 16–17
gable, 19
gable overhangs, 36–39
Greek Revival, 19
hip, 19
mansard, 20
pitch of, 17
rafters for, 40
rake trim, 34–35
ventilation of, 44
venting, 46–47
window, 77
Roof shingles, 138
Roof venting trim, 46–47
decorative, 46–47
Rot-resistant framing, 112
Routers/router tables, 160–161
Routine maintenance, 190

S

Safety
aluminum siding and, 143
deadbolts and, 51, 60
explosure to pressure-treated lumber, 112
nesting sites for wasps and, 36
replacing locksets and, 51
sidelights and, 60
tools, 153
Sanders, 156
Saws, 154, 158–160
bench-top table, 160
circular, 158
coping, 154
hand, 154
jig, 158–159
keyhole, 161
miter, 159
Scratch coat, 146
Screen doors, 56–57
Screened-in gazeboes, 124
Screened-in porches, 57, 111
Secondary entries, 71
Second Empire style, 20
Semitransparent stains, 171
Shingles and shakes, 134–135
inside and outside corners, 135
installing, 134
nailing, 135
preservatives for, 171
Shingle style, 24–25
foundations in, 24
lack of corner boards, 24–25
ornamentation in, 24–25
porches in, 24
roofs in, 24

windows in, 24
Shutters, 78–79
basic designs of, 78
color of, 78
components of, 79
dipping, 78
hardware for, 78
louvered, 67, 78
Sidelights, 18, 60
Soffit vents, 47
types of, 47
Solid color stains, 171
Solid wood bead board, 169
Solid wood trim, 163–165
alternatives to, 166–167
Speed square, 152–153
Spindles, 185
Queen Anne style, 22
repairing, 184–185
Split and resawn shakes, 134
Spray painting, 123
Squares, 152–153
Stained-glass windows, 62
Stains
semitransparent, 171
solid color, 171
Steps, 108–109
handrails for, 108–109
leveling, 108
posts and balustrades for, 109
stone, 109
wood, 109
wraparound, 109
Stone foundation
Shingle style, 24
Victorian style, 25
Storage sheds, 118–121
costs of, 118
plans for, 118
Stucco, 146–147
Sunroom, use of conservatory as, 127
Sunspaces, 126
Surform, 155

T

Texture 1-11, 136
Tin snips, 161
Tongue-and-groove porch boards, 184
replacing, 185
Tools, 152–161
abrasives, 157
block planes, 154–155
cordless drill/driver, 155
files and rasps, 155
levels, 153
power cutting, 158–161
restoration, 161
safety checklist for, 153
sanding and paint removal, 156
saws, 154, 158–160
squares, 152–153
Towers in Queen Anne style, 22, 25
Transom windows, 17, 18, 60, 62, 63
choosing, 63
Transparent water-repellent preservatives, 170–171
Trimwork, replacing damaged, 180–181
Trimwork materials, 162–169
alternatives to solid wood trim, 166–167
matching finish to, 173
panel products, 169
plastic material, 168
solid wood trim, 163–165
Trusses, 40
Try-square, 152

V

Ventiation, of roof, 44
Vents, gable, 46
Vergeboard, 38
Vertical battens, 136
Victorian styles, 20–23, 41, 182
brackets in, 89
color schemes and, 138
friezes in, 84, 85
Italianate style, 20–21
layers of trimwork in, 22
outbuildings in, 121
Queen Anne style, 22–23
Villa style, 20
Vines
for arbors, 129
for pergolas, 68, 69
Vinyl siding, 140–141
cleaning, 141
maintenance and, 190
V-joints, 101

W

Wasps, nesting sites for, 36
Waterproof wood glue, 161
Water tables, 86–87
construction of, 87
pest entrances and, 86
Wind damage to aluminum trim, 177
Windows
Arts and Crafts style, 29
bay, 27
casings for, 74–77
drip caps, 77
seasonal maintenance check, 76
corner, 30
in cupolas, 21
decorative, 62
double-hung, 14, 21, 29
fanlight, 16, 17, 63
Federal, 16–17
Georgian, 14
glass in, 16
Greek Revival, 18–19
Italianate style, 21
keystones for, 16
Modern style, 30
palladium, 27, 63
Queen Anne, 22
roofs for, 77
Shingle style, 24
stained glass, 62
transom, 17, 18, 60, 62, 63
Window stools, repairing, 179
Wood clapboard, 132–133
nailing, 133
types of, 132–133
Wood stabilizer, 161
Wood trim, versus PVC trim, 183
Wraparound stairs, 109
Wrecking bars, 161

Z

Z-channel flashing, 136, 178

CREDITS

page 1: Mark Samu, architect: Bruce Nagel, AIA **page 2:** Jessie Walker **page 5:** *all* John Parsekian/CH **page 6:** Jessie Walker **page 7:** Tony Giammarino/Giammarino & Dworkin **page 8:** *left* Jessie Walker; *right* Tony Giammarino/Giammarino & Dworkin **page 9:** Jessie Walker **page 10:** Tony Giammarino/Giammarino & Dworkin **page 11:** *left* Tony Giammarino/Giammarino & Dworkin; *right* Jessie Walker **page 12:** Phillip Ennis Photography **page 14:** *top* Ken Druse; *bottom* Jessie Walker, home of President Lincoln **page 15:** Eric Roth **page 16:** Amy Wax Orloff/Your Color Source Studios, Inc. **page 17:** *top* Jessie Walker; *bottom* Tony Giammarino/Giammarino & Dworkin **page 16:** *top* Bill Rothschild; *bottom* Jessie Walker, design: Stuart Cohen, FAIA and Julie Hacker, AIA, builder: Barrett Design and Construction **page 19:** Jessie Walker, design: Joseph Blake **page 20:** *top* Tony Giammarino/Giammarino & Dworkin, design: Carden; *center* Tony Giammarino/ Giammarino & Dworkin; *bottom* Jessie Walker, Martindale Bed and Breakfast **page 22:** *top* Jessie Walker, Old World Wisconsin Historic Site; *bottom* Bob Greenspan, stylist: Susan Andrews **page 23:** Jessie Walker **page 24:** Brian Vanden Brink, architect: Thom Rouselle **page 25:** *top* Brian Vanden Brink, architect: Whitten Winkleman Architects; *bottom* Brian Vanden Brink, architect: Polhemus Savery DaSilva Architects **page 26:** Tony Giammarino/Giammarino & Dworkin, design: Maureen & Bob Klein **page 27:** *top* JupiterImages/ Creatas Images; *bottom* Brian Vanden Brink, design: Ron Forest Fences **page 28:** Stan Sudol/CH **page 29:** *top* Bob Greenspan, stylist: Susan Andrews; *center* Jessie Walker, architect: Jim Tharpe; *bottom* Jessie Walker, Country Living House of the Year **page 30:** *top* Tony Giammarino/Giammarino & Dworkin; *bottom* Eric Roth, architect: Mark Hammer Architects **page 31:** Eric Roth **page 32:** Tria Giovan **page 34:** *both* Jessie Walker **page 35:** Bill Rothschild **pages 36–37:** *left* Jessie Walker, home of President Lincoln; *center* Jessie Walker; *right* Tony Giammarino/Giammarino & Dworkin, Hope & Glory Inn **page 38:** Brian Vanden Brink **page 39:** *left & top right* Jessie Walker; *bottom right* Brian Vanden Brink **page 40:** Jessie Walker **page 41:** *top* Anne Gummerson, architect: Andre Fontaine; *bottom* Brian Vanden Brink **page 42:** *top* Tony Giammarino/Giammarino & Dworkin; *bottom* Bill Rothschild **page 43:** Jessie Walker **page 44:** *top* Tony Giammarino/Giammarino & Dworkin; *bottom* Tria Giovan **page 45:** *top & center* courtesy of Calgary Cupola; *bottom* Tony Giammarino/ Giammarino & Dworkin, architect: Bill Prillaman **page 46:** *top* Jessie Walker; *bottom* Jessie Walker, architect: Paul Konstant **page 47:** *top* Merle Henkenius; *bottom* Anne Gummerson **page 48:** Jessie Walker **page 50:** Tria Giovan **page 51:** *left* Jessie Walker; *right* Tria Giovan **page 52:** courtesy of Therma-Tru Doors **page 53:** *all* courtesy of Pella **page 54:** Jessie Walker **page 55:** *top* Mark Lohman; *bottom* Beth Singer, architect: Michael Willoughby/Michael Willoughby & Associates **page 56:** Jessie Walker **page 57:** *all* Bob Greenspan, stylist: Susan Andrews **page 58:** *left* Ken Druse; *right* Tony Giammarino/Giammarino & Dworkin **page 59:** Tria Giovan **pages 60–61:** *both* Phillip Ennis Photography **page 62:** *left* Bob Greenspan, stylist: Susan Andrews; *bottom* Tony Giammarino/Giammarino & Dworkin **page 63:** *left* Tony Giammarino/Giammarino & Dworkin; *right* Anne Gummerson, architect: Laura Thomas/Melville-Thomas Architects **page 64:** *top* Tria Giovan; *bottom* Phillip Ennis Photography **page 65:** Brian Vanden Brink, architect: John Gillespie Architects **page 66:** *top* Mark Lohman; *bottom* courtesy of Pella **page 67:** *top right* www.carolynbates.com; *bottom right* Tria Giovan; *left* Mark Lohman **page 68:** *top left* Bob Greenspan, stylist: Susan Andrews; *bottom right* Mark Lohman **page 69:** Tria Giovan **page 70:** *top* Mark Samu, design: Carpen House; *bottom* Anne Gummerson, architect: David Wiley/Olivieri Shousky and Kiss Architects, landscape architect: Hord Copelan Macht **page 71:** *top right* Tria Giovan; *bottom right* Anne Gummerson, architect: Brennan + Company Architects; *left* Phillip Ennis Photography **page 72:** Brian Vanden Brink **pages 74–75:** *left* Beth Singer, architect: Karen Swanson & Glenda Meads/ Swanson Meads Architects LLC; *center* Brian Vanden Brink; *left* Ken Druse **page 76:** *both* Tony Giammarino/ Giammarino & Dworkin **page 77:** *top* Jessie Walker, architect: Lenore Baigelman; *bottom* Jessie Walker **page 78:** Tony Giammarino/Giammarino & Dworkin **page 79:** *top* Phillip Ennis Photography; *bottom* Tony Giammarino/Giammarino & Dworkin **page 81:** *top right* Phillip Ennis Photography; *bottom right* Mark Samu, design: Schuyler Pond; *left* Jessie Walker, design: Len Mysliewiec Lifespace Design, builder: Rans Custom Builders **page 82:** Beth Singer, architect: Victor Saroki/ Victor Saroki & Associates **page 83:** *top* Brian Vanden Brink, architect: Elliott, Elliott & Norelius Architects; *bottom* Brian Vanden Brink, architect: John Gillespie **page 84:** Brian Vanden Brink **page 85:** *right* Jessie Walker; *bottom left* Stickley Photo•Graphic; *top left* Jessie Walker, Shirley Plantation House **page 86:** *both* Jessie Walker **page 87:** www.carolynbates.com **page 88:** *top* Bob Greenspan, stylist: Susan Andrews; *bottom* Todd Caverly **page 89:** *left* Phillip Ennis Photography; *right* Bob Greenspan, stylist: Susan Andrews **page 90:** Bob Greenspan, stylist: Susan Andrews **page 92:** Phillip Ennis Photography **page 93:** *right* www.carolynbates.com; *left* Jessie Walker **page 94:** *top right* Jessie Walker; *bottom right* melabee m miller, design: Doyle Builders; *left* Brian Vanden Brink, architect: Sally Weston Architects **page 95:** *top right & bottom* Jessie Walker; *top left* Jessie Walker, Martindale Bed and Breakfast **page 96:** Jessie Walker **page 97:** *top right & top left* courtesy of Fypon; *bottom right* Mark Samu **pages 98–99:** *top right* Mark Lohman; *bottom* Tony Giammarino/Giammarino & Dworkin; *left* Jessie Walker; *top center* Jerry Pavia **page 100:** Phillip Ennis Photography **page 101:** *top* Jessie Walker; *bottom* Tony Giammarino/Giammarino & Dworkin, design: Jenny & Bob Saltzman **pages 102–103:** *left* Mark Lohman; *center* Mark Samu, architect: Peter Cook AIA; *right* Jessie Walker, Phipps Inn **page 104:** *right* Bob Greenspan, stylist: Susan Andrews; *bottom left* Tony Giammarino/Giammarino & Dworkin; *top left* Walter Chandoha **page 105:** *top right* Tony Giammarino/Giammarino & Dworkin, design: cedarcrestvictorianinn.com; *bottom right* Tony Giammarino/ Giammarino & Dworkin; *bottom left* Walter Chandoha; *top left* Brian Vanden Brink, architect: John Morris Architects **page 106:** Jessie Walker, architect: Kent Marthaller **page 107:** *left* Jessie Walker; *right* Phillip Ennis Photography **page 108:** *left* www.carolynbates.com; *right* Jessie Walker **page 109:** Tony Giammarino/ Giammarino & Dworkin **page 110:** *top left* Jessie Walker, architect: Tom Greene/Greene and Proppe Design, Inc.; *bottom right* Jessie Walker **page 111:** *top* Mark Samu, architect: Sam Scofield, AIA; *bottom* Mark Samu, design: Rinaldi Associates **page 112:** Jessie Walker **page 113:** Mark Lohman **page 114:** Jessie Walker **page 116:** *top* Jessie Walker, architect: Scott Javore Architects; *bottom* Tony Giammarino/Giammarino & Dworkin, design: Carden **page 117:** Tony Giammarino/Giammarino & Dworkin **page 118:** Donna Chiarelli/CH **page 119:** *top* Jessie Walker; *center* Tony Giammarino/Giammarino & Dworkin; *bottom* Simon McBride/Redcover.com **page 120:** Jessie Walker **page 121:** *top right* Tony Giammarino/Giammarino & Dworkin; *center right* Mark Samu, design: Schuyler Pond; *bottom right* Tony Giammarino/Giammarino & Dworkin. design: George Wilbur; *left* Tony Giammarino/Giammarino & Dworkin, design: Carden **page 122:** Jessie Walker **page 123:** *top* James Mejuto; *bottom* www.carolynbates.com **page 124:** Mark Samu, design: Jamesport Showhouse **page 125:** *top* Mark Samu, design: Pascucci-Deslisle Interiors; *bottom* Tony Giammarino/Giammarino & Dworkin, Edgewood Plantation Inn **page 126:** *top* Tony Giammarino/Giammarino & Dworkin; *bottom* Phillip Ennis Photography **page 127:** Jessie Walker, architect/ builder: Tom Swarthout **page 128:** Phillip Clayton-Thomas, garden design: Karen & Frank Capillupo **page 129:** *top right* Donna Chiarelli/CH; *bottom right* Tony Giammarino/Giammarino & Dworkin; *left* Jerry Pavia, garden design: Joann Romano **page 130:** Beth Singer, architect: Victor Saroki/Victor Saroki & Associates **page 132:** *top* Ken Druse; *bottom* Phillip Ennis Photography **page 133:** Stickley Photo•Graphic **page 134:** Jessie Walker **page 135:** Ken Druse **page 136:** *bottom right* Mark Lohman; *bottom left* Walter Chandoha; *top left* Jessie Walker **page 137:** Tria Giovan **page 138:** Tony Giammarino/Giammarino & Dworkin **page 139:** *top* Tony Giammarino/Giammarino & Dworkin; *bottom* Tony Giammarino/Giammarino & Dworkin, design: Carden **pages 140–141:** *all* courtesy of Crane Performance Siding **page 142:** *left* Robert Anderson; *right* Beth Singer, architect: Michael Guthrie/Vantine/ Guthrie Studio of Architecture **page 143:** Bob Greenspan, stylist: Susan Andrews **pages 144–145:** *both* courtesy of CertainTeed **page 146:** Phillip Ennis Photography **page 147:** *top* Tony Giammarino/Giammarino & Dworkin; *bottom* Jessie Walker **page 148:** Beth Singer, architect: David Lubin/Lubin & Associates **page 149:** Beth Singer, architect: Victor Saroki/Victor Saroki & Associates **page 150:** Mark Lohman **page 152:** Gary David Gold/CH **page 153:** *top* Neil Barrett/CH; *bottom* John Parsekian/CH **page 154:** *A, D & E* Neil Barrett/ CH; *C* Gary David Gold/CH; *F* John Parsekian/CH **pages 155–156:** *all* Gary David Gold/CH **page 157:** Neil Barrett/CH **pages 158–159:** *all* Gary David Gold/CH **page 160:** *top* Neal Barrett/CH; *bottom* John Parsekian/ CH **page 161:** Neal Barrett/CH **page 162:** *top* Neal Barrett/CH; *bottom* Tony Giammarino/ Giammarino & Dworkin, design: Jenny & Bob Saltzman **page 163:** Jessie Walker **page 164:** Neal Barrett/CH **page 165:** Jessie Walker, Prairie Crossing **pages 166–167:** *all* courtesy of CertainTeed **page 168:** *both* courtesy of Fypon **page 169:** Jessie Walker **page 170:** *top* Phillip Ennis Photography; *bottom* Stickley Photo•Graphic **page 171:** Mark Samu, architect: David Andreozzi, AIA **page 172:** *top* Jessie Walker; *bottom* Tony Giammarino/Giammarino & Dworkin **page 173:** Jessie Walker **page 174:** www.carolynbates.com **page 176:** *top right* John Parsekian/CH; *bottom right* Merle Henkenius; *left both* National Paint & Coatings Association **page 177:** Jessie Walker **page 178:** *top* John Parsekian/CH; *bottom* Tony Giammarino/Giammarino & Dworkin **page 179:** *top* Jessie Walker, architect: Scott Javore Architects; *bottom* Jessie Walker **page 180:** Tony Giammarino/Giammarino & Dworkin **pages 181–182:** *all* Jessie Walker **page 183:** *top* courtesy of Fypon; *bottom* Jessie Walker **page 184:** *both* Roger Bruhn **page 185:** *top* Tony Giammarino/ Giammarino & Dworkin; *bottom* Roger Bruhn **page 186:** *left* Roger Holmes; *right* Roger Bruhn **page 187:** Tria Giovan **page 188:** Tony Giammarino/Giammarino & Dworkin **page 189:** *both* Tony Giammarino/Giammarino & Dworkin **page 190:** Jessie Walker **page 191:** *left* Tria Giovan; *right* Jessie Walker, architect: Kent Marthaller **page 192:** courtesy of Therma-Tru Doors **page 193:** courtesy of Fypon **page 194:** courtesy of Pella **page 195:** courtesy of Crane Performance Siding **pages 196–197:** *both* courtesy of Fypon

Have a home improvement, decorating, or gardening project? Look for these and other fine Creative Homeowner books wherever books are sold.

Enhance a room's aesthetic appeal using trimwork. 550+ color photos, illustrations. 240 pp.; 8½" x 10⅞"
BOOK #: 277500

1001 IDEAS FOR TRIMWORK

Design resource for every room in your home. Over 1,080 color photos, illos. 256 pp.; 8½" x 10⅞"
BOOK #: 279402

Guide to designing and building decks. Over 650 color photos. 288 pp.; 8½" x 10⅞"
BOOK #: 277168

Learn everything about pools, from planning to installation. 300 color photos. 224 pp.; 8½" x 10⅞"
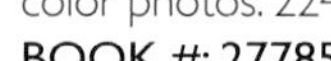
BOOK #: 277853

Build landscape structures from concrete, brick, stone. 500+ color illustrations. 240 pp.; 8½" x 10⅞"
BOOK #: 277997

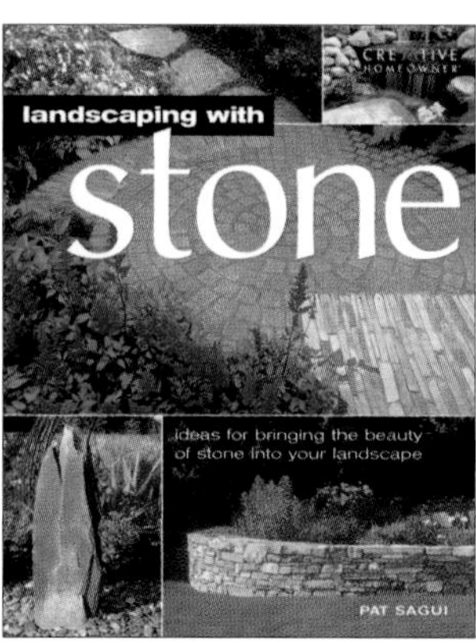

Enhance your landscape by using stone in its design. 375+ photos, illustrations. 224 pp.; 8½" x 10⅞"
BOOK #: 274172

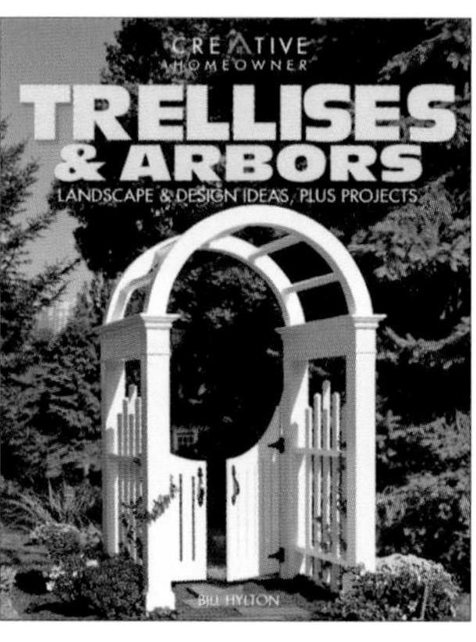

Design ideas, planning advice, and projects. 460+ color photos, illustrations. 160 pp.; 8½" x 10⅞"
BOOK #: 274804

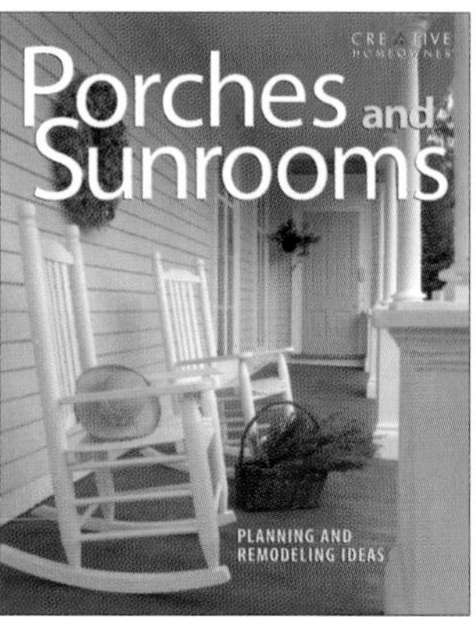

Learn how to add on a porch or sunroom. 350+ color photos, illustrations. 224 pp.; 8½" x 10⅞"
BOOK #: 277977

Design solutions for every room in the house. 500+ color photos. 320 pp.; 8½" x 10⅞"
BOOK #: 279323

Remodeling makeovers, case studies, and more. 250+ color photos. 224 pp.; 9¼" x 10⅞"
BOOK #: 279275

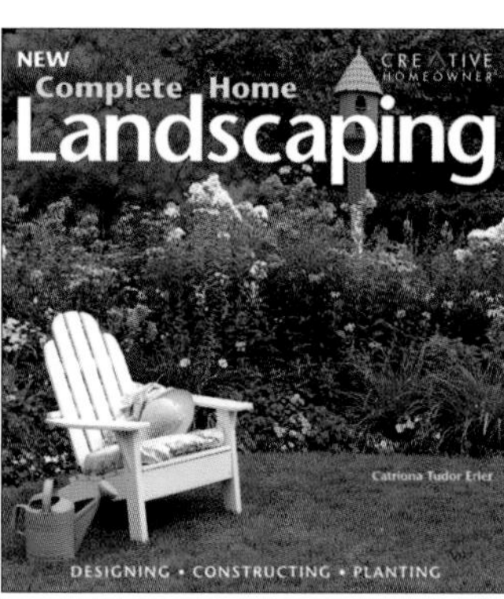

Complete guide to designing and planting with emphasis on solving problems. 870+ photos and illustrations. 384 pp.; 9" x 10" paper
BOOK #: 274610

Lavishly illustrated with portraits of over 100 flowering plants; planting and care tips; 500+ color photos. 208 pp.; 9" x 10"
BOOK #: 274032

For more information, and to order direct, go to **www.creativehomeowner.com**